PIERCED FOR OUR TRANSGRESSIONS

PETER LENGWE

All Scripture quotations are taken from the New King James Version® (NKJV).

Printed in the United States of America

ISBN:
Softcover: 978-1-972299-75-3
Hardback: 978-1-972299-76-0
eBook: 978-1-972299-74-6

For permission requests, visit and write to the publisher at:

Peter Lengwe | THE BREAD OF LIFE GLOBAL MINISTRIES

TABLE OF CONTENTS

PREFACE

This book was born out of a deep desire to understand the final days of Jesus Christ—not just through tradition, but through Scripture, history, and the Jewish calendar. For years, Passion Week has been seen by Christians around the world, but many do not realize how precise and prophetic the timeline truly is.

By aligning the events of Jesus 'final week with the Hebrew calendar and the timing of the Jewish feasts, we begin to see more clearly the divine plan that was unfolding. Every step He took, every hour that passed, fulfilled a purpose written long before He walked the dusty roads of Jerusalem.

This book is not only for believers but also for the curious, the skeptical, and the seeking. It is an invitation to reconsider what we think we know—and to marvel at the exactness of God's timing in the life, death, and resurrection of Jesus.

Dedication

To the One who walked the road to Calvary,

whose love was measured in blood and time— this work is for You.

And to every reader who dares to look deeper,
may these pages lead you closer to truth,

and closer to Him.

INTRODUCTION

To understand the events leading up to the final days of the Lord Jesus Christ's ministry on earth, we must carefully examine all four Gospels—Matthew, Mark, Luke, and John. These books, known as the Good News, each offer a unique perspective, and when harmonized, they provide a fuller picture of Jesus 'final week.

This important period begins with His triumphal entry into Jerusalem and continues through to His crucifixion which occured on the day of the Passover feast which was considered a high sabbath because it falls not on the Sabbath day (Saturday). This is the main point of this book why I felt led by the Spirit to write and prove the exact day of the Lord Jesus Christ's crucifixion and His resurrection according to the Word of God and the Jewish calendar. These last days were not only the final steps of His earthly ministry —they were the fulfillment of prophecy, the climax of His mission, and the turning point of history.

The first clear mention of Jesus going to Jerusalem to suffer, be killed, and rise again on the third day is found in the Gospel of Matthew. This moment marked a turning point in His ministry.

It began with a powerful conversation between Jesus and His disciples at Caesarea Philippi:

"When Jesus came into the coasts of Caesarea Philippi, He asked His disciples, saying, 'Whom do men say that I the Son of man am?'

And they said, 'Some say that thou art John the Baptist: some, Elijah; and others, Jeremiah, or one of the prophets.'

He saith unto them, 'But who say ye that I am?'

And Simon Peter answered and said, 'Thou art the Christ, the

Son of the living God.'

And Jesus answered and said unto him, 'Blessed art thou, Simon Bar-jona: for flesh and blood hath not revealed it unto thee, but My Father which is in heaven.

And I say also unto thee, that thou art Peter, and upon this rock I will build My church; and the gates of hell shall not prevail against it.

And I will give unto thee the keys of the kingdom of heaven: and whatsoever thou shalt bind on earth shall be bound in heaven: and whatsoever thou shalt loose on earth shall be loosed in heaven.'

Then charged He His disciples that they should tell no man that He was Jesus the Christ.

From that time forth began Jesus to shew unto His disciples, how that He must go unto Jerusalem, and suffer many things of the elders and chief priests and scribes, and be killed, and be raised again the third day."

— Matthew 16:13–21 (KJV)

This revelation was not just a warning—it was a declaration of purpose. From that point forward, Jesus began preparing His disciples for what was to come. His journey to Jerusalem was not accidental; it was divine destiny. The path He would walk was prophesied and foreshadowed in the feasts and patterns of the Old Testament.

In this book, we will walk that path with Him—step by step—through the lens of the Jewish calendar, historical context, and the harmony of the Gospels.

Now, before outlining the last final days of the Lord Jesus 'ministry and life on earth, it is important to explain a key concept often misunderstood: the meaning of "the third day" or "three days and three nights." To utterly understand this phrase—a Hebrew idiom—we must go back to the very beginning, to the creation of time itself.

The book of Genesis records:

"And God saw the light, that it was good: and God divided the light from the darkness.

And God called the light Day, and the darkness He called Night. And the evening and the morning were the first day."
— Genesis 1:4–5 (KJV)

This passage shows how God defines a full day: "the evening and the morning" make up one day—a complete 24-hour cycle. In other words, the day begins at sunset, not at midnight or sunrise. From sunset to sunrise is the night, and from sunrise to sunset is the daylight part.

Together, they form a full Hebrew day.

So, in the Hebrew reckoning of time, a day runs from sunset to sunset—from 6:00 PM to 6:00 PM by our modern clocks. This divine pattern, set by God at creation, is the basis for how time is seen in the Jewish calendar.

Understanding this is crucial, especially when we consider Jesus 'words about being in the heart of the earth for "three days and three nights."

Without the correct biblical view of a day, we can easily misunderstand the timeline of His death and resurrection.

Let us look at another Scripture that supports this understanding of a day in the Hebrew calendar:

"Go, gather together all the Jews that are present in Shushan, and fast for me; neither eat nor drink for three days, night or day. My maids and I will fast likewise. And so will I go in to the king, which is not according to the law; and if I perish, I perish."

—Esther 4:16 (NKJV)

In this passage, Queen Esther calls for a fast of three days, night, and day. Her words reflect an understanding of the divinely set up Hebrew day: beginning at evening (night) and followed by morning (day)—just as it was from creation. This reinforces the biblical reckoning of time that Jesus and all Jews of His time lived by.

Now, it is important to highlight the key difference between the Hebrew calendar—set up by God—and the modern calendar used today, which man set up.

- God's calendar begins each day at sunset (around 6:00 PM) and ends at sunset the following day. This system is based on the solar-lunar cycle, which combines the movements of the sun and the moon—a pattern set up by God in Genesis.

- The Gregorian calendar day begins at midnight and ends at the next midnight. This system follows a purely solar-based cycle, detached from the original biblical model.

The Gregorian calendar was introduced by Pope Gregory XIII of the Roman Catholic Church in 1582 and gradually became the standard calendar used around the world today. While it serves civil and global purposes, it does not align with the timekeeping system God instituted at creation and followed throughout Scripture.

Understanding this distinction is vital when studying the final days of Jesus 'life. Without viewing His death, burial, and resurrection through the lens of the Hebrew calendar, we risk misinterpreting the timeline He Himself instituted.

CHAPTER ONE: THE TRIUMPHAL ENTRY OF THE REJECTED KING

As I begin this first chapter, my focus is to accurately prove the timeline of the last days of the Lord Jesus Christ's life and ministry on Earth, according to the divine ordination of God's days and time as revealed in Genesis 1:3–5. This was discussed in the introduction, and it is the same divine timeline that God entrusted to the Hebrews.

This timeline was also used and seen during the days of the Lord Jesus Christ. There are nine recorded occurrences where the Lord Jesus Christ predicted His suffering, death, and resurrection:

- Three are in the book of Matthew:
    - Matthew 16:22
    - Matthew 17:23
    - Matthew 20:19
- Two are in the book of Mark:
    - Mark 9:31

    - Mark 10:34
- Four are in the book of Luke:
    - Luke 9:22
    - Luke 18:33
    - Luke 24:7
    - Luke 24:46

The record of the last days of the Lord Jesus Christ is in the four Holy Gospels, which should more accurately rendered as "Good News" or "Good Tidings" about the Christ (the Messiah). The term gospel does not originate from the Greek language; rather, it is a coined word by translators, derived from the Anglo-Saxon Godspell. The correct translation from the original Greek text is joyful tidings. Therefore, the Gospel of Matthew should more accurately be rendered as The Good News of the Messiah According to Matthew.

As I mentioned earlier, my goal is to prove a timeline of the last days of the Lord Jesus. With that in mind, I will be referencing all four Gospel accounts. After carefully studying each of the Gospels, I find it proper to begin with the book of Luke, where the Lord and His disciples begin their journey to Jerusalem through Jericho. Along the way, they meet Zacchaeus, and after dining at his house, the Lord Jesus proceeds to tell the parable of the minas. When He finishes, He continues His journey toward Jerusalem with His disciples.

"When He had said this, He went on ahead, going up to Jerusalem."

—Luke 19:28 NKJV

It is important to understand that there are two triumphal entries. The first is in Matthew 21:1– 12, and the second is in Luke 19:28–40. The account in John 12:12–15 corresponds with the one in Luke. There is no contradiction here—the Word of God does not contradict itself; rather, it confirms itself. When you examine the context of these two triumphal entries closely, you will clearly see and understand the distinction I am making.

The first triumphal entry

"Now when they drew near Jerusalem, and came to Bethphage, at the Mount of Olives, then Jesus sent two disciples, saying to them, "Go into the village opposite you, and immediately you will find a donkey tied, and a colt with her. Loose them and bring them to Me. And if anyone says anything to you, you shall say, 'The Lord has need of them, 'and immediately he will send them." All this was done that it might be fulfilled which was spoken by the prophet, saying: "Tell the daughter of Zion, 'Behold, your King is coming to you, Lowly, and sitting on a donkey, A colt, the foal of a donkey.'"""

Matthew 21:1-5 NKJV

And the second triumphal entry

"When He had said this, He went on ahead, going up to Jerusalem. And it came to pass, when He drew near to Bethphage and Bethany, at the mountain called Olivet, that He sent two of His disciples, saying, "Go into the village opposite you, where as you enter you will find a colt tied, on which no one has ever sat. Loose it and bring it here. And if anyone asks you, 'Why are you loosing it? 'thus you shall say to him, 'Because the Lord has need of it."'So those who were sent went their way and found it just as He had said to them. But as they were loosing the colt, the owners of it said to them, "Why are you loosing the colt?" And they said, "The Lord has need of him." Then they brought him to Jesus. And they threw their own clothes on the colt, and they set Jesus on him. Then, as He was now drawing near the descent of the Mount of Olives, the whole multitude of the disciples began to rejoice and praise God with a loud voice for all the mighty works they had seen, saying: '"Blessed is the King who comes in the name of the Lord! 'Peace in heaven and glory in the highest!" And some of the Pharisees called to Him from the crowd, "Teacher, rebuke Your disciples.""

— Luke 19:28-35, 37-39 NKJV

The first notable difference between the two triumphal entries is in the instructions the Lord Jesus gives about the animals. In the first triumphal entry, recorded in Matthew 21:2 (NKJV), Jesus says to the two disciples:

"Go into the village opposite you, and immediately you will find a donkey tied, and a colt with her. Loose them and bring them to Me."

In the second triumphal entry, recorded in Luke 19:30 (NKJV), He again sends two disciples, saying:

"Go into the village opposite you, where as you enter you will find a colt tied, on which no one has ever sat. Loose it and bring it here."

The key difference lies in the number of animals mentioned. In Matthew's account, two animals—a donkey and a colt. (A colt is a young donkey.) However, in Luke's account, only a colt.

Now, here is the reason for the difference: the first triumphal entry in Matthew 21:2 was to fulfill prophecy, specifically the one spoken by the prophet Zechariah. Matthew himself makes this clear by referencing Zechariah 9:9, which says:

"Rejoice greatly, O daughter of Zion! Shout, O daughter of Jerusalem!

Behold, your King is coming to you; He is just and having salvation, Lowly and riding on a donkey,

A colt, the foal of a donkey." Zechariah 9:9, NKJV

This prophecy explicitly mentions both a donkey and a colt, which is why Matthew records the presence of two animals during that triumphal entry.

Furthermore, another notable difference between the two triumphal entries is the response of the people. In the first triumphal entry, recorded in Matthew 21, the event seemed unexpected:

"And when He had come into Jerusalem, all the city was moved, saying, 'Who is this? 'So, the multitudes said, 'This is Jesus, the prophet from

Nazareth of Galilee.'"
—Matthew 21:10–11, NKJV

In contrast, the second triumphal entry appears that the people were expecting the Lord Jesus. John 12 describes a crowd that was not only expecting Jesus but actively went out to meet Him:

"The next day a great multitude that had come to the feast, when they heard that Jesus was coming to Jerusalem, took branches of palm trees, and went out to meet Him, and cried out:

'Hosanna!

Blessed is He who comes in the name of the Lord! The King of Israel!'"

—John 12:12–13, NKJV

The other notable difference between the first triumphal entry (in Matthew 21) and the second (in Luke 19 and John 12) is the timing. The second triumphal entry appears to have taken place on the day of the feast:

This event traditionally is Palm Sunday. In contrast, the first triumphal entry, as recorded in Matthew, appears to have occurred two days earlier.

The last, but not the least, notable difference between the two triumphal entries is that in the first entry, the Lord Jesus Christ went into the Temple and cleansed it.

"Then Jesus went into the temple of God and drove out all those who bought and sold in the temple and overturned the tables of the money changers and the seats of those who sold doves.

And He said to them, 'It is written, "My house shall be called a house of prayer," but you have made it a "den of thieves."' Then the blind and the lame came to Him in the temple, and He healed them.

But when the chief priests and scribes saw the wonderful things that He did, and the children crying out in the temple and saying, 'Hosanna to the Son of David! 'they were indignant, and said to Him, 'Do You hear what these are saying? 'And Jesus said to them, 'Yes. Have you never read, "Out of the mouth of babes and nursing infants You have perfected praise"?'

Then He left them and went out of the city to Bethany, and He lodged there."

— Matthew 21:12–17, NKJV

Following His triumphal entry into Jerusalem, the Lord Jesus Christ entered the Temple and His heart was grieved by what He saw. The sacred place, intended to be a house of prayer, had been reduced to a place of commerce and corruption. Moved by holy indignation, He cleansed the Temple, driving out those who had defiled it. Afterward, He withdrew to Bethany.

In contrast, during His second approach to the city, the tone shifted from confrontation to compassion. As He drew near and beheld Jerusalem, He wept over it—mourning the spiritual blindness of its people and the coming judgment they had unknowingly invited:

"Now as He drew near, He saw the city and wept over it, saying,

'If you had known, even you, especially in this your day, the things that make for your peace! But now they are hidden from your eyes. "For days will come upon you when your

enemies will build an embankment around you, surround you and close you in on every side, and level you, and your children within you, to the ground; and they will not leave in you one stone upon another, because you did not know the time of your visitation."'

— Luke 19:43-44 NKJV

From the time of His first triumphal entry until the evening of the Last Supper, Jesus lodged in Bethany, staying with His dear friend Lazarus

(Whom He had raised from the dead) and his two sisters with His disciples. Bethany became His place of rest, retreat, and preparation in the final days before the cross.

In conclusion of Chapter One: Based on what I have gathered from the Gospels accounts, the first triumphal entry took place on Friday, the 8th of Nisan, which would correspond to April 1st on the modern calendar. Saturday, the 9th of Nisan, was the Sabbath, followed by Sunday, the 10th of Nisan, or April 3rd, which was Palm Sunday—the day of the second triumphal entry.

Reflection

These two triumphal entries, though different in detail, reveal the divine precision of God's prophetic timeline. Nothing about the Lord Jesus Christ's final journey to Jerusalem was by chance—each event fulfilled Scripture and unfolded according to the will of the Father. The first entry, marked by humility, and the second, marked by public celebration, both point to the identity of Jesus as the promised Messiah. As we reflect on these moments, we are not merely observers of history but participants in the ongoing call to recognize and worship our King. Let our hearts echo the cry of the crowds: "Hosanna! Blessed is He who comes in the name of the

Lord!" May this foundation deepen our understanding as we continue to trace the final days of Christ's earthly ministry in the chapters ahead.

CHAPTER TWO: THREE ANOINTING (DIVINE ANTICIPATION)

In this chapter, I want to focus on the events that took place on the second day—the 9th of Nisan, which was a Sabbath day (our Saturday). As shown in Chapter One, the first triumphal entry occurred on the 8th of Nisan, a Friday. Now, we turn our attention to what followed—what happened on the Sabbath, the day in between t he two triumphal entries.

As the Gospel of Matthew records, after the triumphal entry into Jerusalem, the Lord Jesus returned to Bethany, which became His place of lodging during the final days leading up to His crucifixion. He stayed at the home of Lazarus and his sisters, Mary and Martha. Each day, Jesus would leave Bethany in the morning and go into Jerusalem to teach in the temple. Then, at sunset, He would return to Bethany with His disciples.

"Then He left them and went out of the city to Bethany, and He lodged there."

— Matthew 21:17

There are two notable events that took place when Jesus returned to Bethany after His triumphal entry into Jerusalem. These events in the Gospel of John occurred six days before the Passover, which places them on the 10th of Nisan, a Sabbath day (Saturday).

"Then, six days before the Passover, Jesus came to Bethany, where Lazarus was who had been dead, whom He had raised from the dead. There they made Him a supper; and Martha served, but Lazarus was one of those who sat at the table with Him. Then Mary took a pound of very costly oil of spikenard, anointed the feet of Jesus, and wiped His feet with her hair.

And the house was filled with the fragrance of the oil. But one of His disciples, Judas Iscariot, Simon's son, who would betray Him, said, 'Why was this fragrant oil not sold for three hundred denarii and given to the poor? 'This he said, not that he cared for the poor, but because he was a thief, and had the money box; and he used to take what was put in it. But Jesus said, 'Let her alone; she has kept this for the day of My burial. For the poor you have with you always, but Me you do not have always.'"

— (John 12:1–8, NKJV)

There are three anointing of the Lord Jesus, and three suppers recorded in the Gospels. As I mentioned in Chapter One, the Word of God does not contradict itself—it confirms itself. When studying Scripture, it is essential to look closely at the context. Sometimes, events, miracles, or sayings of the Lord may appear similar, but upon deeper examination, the location, the people involved, or the timing may be different. In some accounts, the names of people or place is mentioned, while in other cases not mentioned. These details matter. They help us rightly divide the Word of truth and avoid confusion as we study the life and ministry of Jesus.

"Then, six days before the Passover, Jesus came to Bethany, where

Lazarus was who had been dead, whom He had raised from the dead. There they made Him a supper; and Martha served, but Lazarus was one of those who sat at the table with Him. Then Mary took a pound of very costly oil of spikenard, anointed the feet of Jesus, and wiped His feet with her hair. And the house was filled with the fragrance of the oil. But one of His disciples, Judas Iscariot, Simon's son, who would betray Him, said, "Why was this fragrant oil not sold for three hundred denarii and given to the poor?" This he said, not that he cared for the poor, but because he was a thief, and had the money box; and he used to take what was put in it."

—John 12:1-6 NKJV

For instance, let us take a closer look at the anointing recorded in the Gospel of John. In this account, the location is in Bethany, at the house of Lazarus, Mary, and Martha. The person who anoints Him is Mary.she anointed the feet of the Lord Jesus and wiped them with her hair.

Furthermore, one of the disciples, Judas Iscariot, by name, the son of Simon, distinguishing him from the other Judas who was also among the disciples. John's Gospel also reveals Judas's motives, exposing his hypocrisy and greed. This act of Mary reflects on her personal intimacy, and devotion to the Lord Jesus Christ, something to be emulated by all believers in Christ the Lord.No wonder she was the first one to see the Lord Jesus Christ after His resurrection.

Now let us cross-reference this with another anointing recorded in the Gospel of Luke:

"Then one of the Pharisees asked Him to eat with him. And He went to the Pharisee's house and sat down to eat. And behold, a woman in the city who was a sinner, when she knew that Jesus sat at the table in the Pharisee's house, brought an alabaster flask of fragrant oil, and stood at His feet behind Him weeping; and she began to wash His feet with her tears, and wiped them with the hair of her head; and she kissed His feet and anointed them with the fragrant oil. Now when the Pharisee

who had invited Him saw this, he spoke to himself, saying, 'This Man, if He were a prophet, would know who and what manner of woman this is who is touching Him, for she is a sinner.'"

— *(Luke 7:36–39, NKJV)*

This passage presents a different context altogether. The setting is not Bethany, but rather the house of a Pharisee, whose name we later learn is Simon.We are not told the name of the woman but described as a sinner—known in the city for her sinful lifestyle. She also anoints Jesus's feet, weeping and wiping them with her hair, but the details, the tone of the event, and the response from the host are clearly distinct from the account in the gospel of John 12:1-6

She brought with her an alabaster flask of fragrant oil—a different type from the one used by Mary in the Gospel of John. We given a detailed and moving description of how she anointed the Lord:

- First, she stood behind Him at His feet, weeping.
- She began to wash His feet with her tears.
- Then she wiped His feet with her hair.
- She kissed His feet repeatedly.
- And finally, she anointed them with the fragrant oil.

This act of devotion was deeply emotional and personal. It was an expression of repentance, love, and humility.

Let us now consider yet another account of the Lord Jesus anointing, this time recorded in the Gospel of Mark. This passage deepens the perspective and helps further support the point I have been making:

"And being in Bethany at the house of Simon the leper, as He sat at the table, a woman came having an alabaster flask of very costly oil of spikenard. Then she broke the flask and poured it on His head. But there

were some who were indignant among themselves, and said, 'Why was this fragrant oil wasted? For it might have been sold for more than three hundred denarii and given to the poor. 'And they criticized her sharply."

— Mark 14:3–5, NKJV

In this account, the location is again Bethany, but this time at the house of Simon the leper—a different Simon than the Pharisee in Luke 7. The woman is unnamed, and the anointing is on Jesus's head, not His feet. The oil specified as very costly spikenard, similar in type to Mary's oil in John 12, but this detail alone does not make it the same event.

Another notable point is the reaction of those present. Rather than Judas alone speaking (as in John), in Mark we are told that some among the group were indignant, criticizing the act and calling it a waste.

This comparison reinforces the truth that these are not conflicting stories, but rather separate moments, each carrying its own prophetic and spiritual significance. As always, Scripture confirms itself, and a careful study reveals harmony rather than contradiction.

In summary of the three anointing of the Lord Jesus Christ. Let us look at the three responses of the Lord.

1. John 12:1–8

Mary anoints Jesus's feet at Lazarus's house in Bethany

Jesus's response:

But Jesus said" Let her alone; she has kept this for the day of My burial. For the poor you have with you always, but Me you do not have always."

— John 12:7–8, NKJV

Significance:

Jesus affirms Mary's actions as prophetic preparation for His burial. He defends her against Judas's criticism and draws a powerful distinction between temporal charity and recognizing the presence of the Messiah in a moment of divine significance.

2. Luke 7:36–50

The sinful woman anoints Jesus's feet at Simon the Pharisee's house

Jesus's response:

Then He turned to the woman and said to Simon, "Do you see this woman? I entered your house; you gave Me no water for My feet, but she has washed My feet with her tears and wiped them with the hair of her head. You gave Me no kiss, but this woman has not ceased to kiss My feet since the time I came in. You did not anoint My head with oil, but this woman has

anointed My feet with fragrant oil. Therefore I say to you, her sins, which are many, are forgiven, for she loved much. But to whom little is forgiven, the same loves little.""

— Luke 7:44-47 NKJV

Significance:

Jesus uses this moment to teach about forgiveness and love. He contrasts the cold hospitality of Simon with the extravagant love of the woman. Her act becomes a teaching moment on grace— her faith and repentance lead to forgiveness.

3. Mark 14:3–9

(Also)

Matthew 26:6–13

An unnamed woman anoints Jesus's head at Simon the leper's house

Jesus's response:

"But Jesus said, "Let her alone. Why do you trouble her? She has done an excellent work for Me. "For you have the poor with you always, and whenever you wish you may do them good; but Me you do not have always. She has done what she could. She has come beforehand to anoint My body for burial. Assuredly, I say to you, wherever this gospel is preached in the whole world, what this woman has done will also be told as a memorial to her."

— Mark 14:6–9 NKJV

Significance:

Once again, Jesus connects the anointing to His upcoming death and burial. He calls her act a "good work" and shows it as a memorial—ensuring her actions will read alongside the preaching of the gospel.

CHAPTER THREE: THE THREE SUPPERS

As we continue tracing the final days of our Lord Jesus Christ, we now focus on a series of meals—three important suppers—that the Gospels record. Though they may seem similar on the surface, each supper reveals something unique about Jesus, the people around Him, and the mission He was soon to fulfill.

These three suppers happened in separate places, with different people, and for distinct reasons. But they all carry a common thread: they prepare the way for the cross, and each one reveals a different aspect of God's Grace.

1. The Supper in Bethany – A Moment of Worship

"Then, six days before the Passover, Jesus came to Bethany, where Lazarus was who had been dead, whom He had raised from the dead. There they made Him a supper; and Martha served, but Lazarus was one of those who sat at the table with Him."

John 12:1-2 NKJV

This supper took place six days before the Passover at the home of Lazarus, Mary, and Martha in Bethany, where Jesus stayed during His final week. After His triumphal entry, He returned here to rest.

During the supper, Mary anointed Jesus's feet with costly oil, wiping them with her hair. Her act of love was prophetic—Jesus said she was preparing Him for His burial:

"But Jesus said, "Let her alone; she has kept this for the day of My burial."

— John 12:7 NKJV

This supper was with intimacy, worship, and preparation. It reminds us that those who genuinely love Jesus will give Him their absolute best, even when others do not Understand.

2. The Supper at the Pharisee's House – A Lesson on Forgiveness

Luke 7:36–50

During this supper, Jesus dined at Simon the Pharisee's house. During the meal, a woman unnamed but known in the city as a sinner came in, weeping. She washed Jesus's feet with her tears, wiped them with her hair, and anointed His feet with oil.

Simon judged her in his heart, but Jesus responded with a powerful lesson:

"Therefore, I say to you, her sins, which are many, are forgiven, for she loved much. But to whom little is forgiven, the same loves little.""

— Luke 7:47 NKJV

This supper revealed that true forgiveness is available to those who come to Jesus with a repentant heart. It also exposed the difference between outward religion and inward transformation.

3. The Last Supper – A Covenant Established

Matthew 26, Mark 14, Luke 22, John 13–17

On the night before His crucifixion, Jesus gathered with His disciples in an upper room in Jerusalem to eat the Passover meal. This was no ordinary supper—it was the beginning of a new covenant.

At this meal:

- Jesus washed His disciples 'feet, teaching humility, and service.
- Jesus' spoke of the betrayal and instituted communion, offering bread and wine as symbols of His body and blood.

"This is My blood of the new covenant, which is shed for many

for the remission of sins."

— Matthew 26:28, NKJV

This was the most sacred of all suppers—where Jesus revealed the full meaning of His mission and prepared His followers for what was to come.

Reflection

Each of these meals shows a different side of Jesus:

- In Bethany, He is the honored King.
- In Galilee, He is the forgiving, Savior.
- In Jerusalem, He is the sacrificial Lamb.

As we follow His final days, may we see ourselves at each table—worshipping like Mary, repenting like the woman in Luke, and receiving His covenant at the Last Supper.

CHAPTER FOUR: WEEPING OVER HIS OWN

As Jesus approached Jerusalem on the 10th Nisan, which is Sunday, the sounds of celebration echoed in the air. Crowds shouted "Hosanna! Clothes laid on the road. Palm branches waved in the wind.

But the King was not smiling. Instead, He wept.

And not just with a single tear, but with deep, soul-wrenching sorrow.

"Now as He drew near, He saw the city and wept over it,"

— Luke 19:41 NKJV

The Greek word used here for "wept" is ἔκλαυσεν (eklausēn)—not a silent shedding of tears, but a loud, public sobbing. The same word used in John 11:35, where Jesus wept over Lazarus, showing a depth of emotion that is both divine and profoundly human.

This moment tells us something staggering:

The Son of God broke down in tears—right at the city gates.

"If Only You Had Known..."

"If you had known, even you, especially in this your day, the things that make for your peace! But now they are hidden from your eyes."

— Luke 19:42

Jesus speaks as a heartbroken prophet, as One who came offering peace—shalom, a word far deeper than the absence of conflict. Shalom meant wholeness, healing, salvation. And "this your day" refers to something more than just a calendar date.

It was their moment of divine visitation—a time prophesied hundreds of years earlier by Daniel:

"Know and understand this: From the issuing of the decree to restore and rebuild Jerusalem... until the Anointed One, the ruler, comes, there will be seven 'sevens,' and sixty-two 'sevens.'"

— Daniel 9:25 (NIV)

That prophecy counted down the very day Messiah would enter Jerusalem—and here He was. Right on time.

But they missed it.

Prophecy Fulfilled, Rejected by the Blind:

""Rejoice greatly, O daughter of Zion! Shout, O daughter of Jerusalem! Behold, your King is coming to you; He is just and having salvation, Lowly and riding on a donkey, A colt, the foal of a donkey."

— Zechariah 9:9 NKJV

This prophecy in Zechariah 9:9 was the fulfillment of Jesus' triumphal entry into Jerusalem. He rode into the city not on a warhorse, but on a donkey, a symbol of peace. The people had shouted the right words—"Blessed is He who comes in the name of the Lord!" (Psalm 118:26)—but they misunderstood the kind of salvation He came to bring.

"But now they are hidden from your eyes..."

— (Luke 19:42)

The verb ἐκρύβη (ekrybē) means "to be veiled, concealed."

Their eyes were spiritually shut. They saw a prophet, but not the Messiah, and could not behold the Lamb of God—the very one who came take away the sin (rebellion singular) of the world (John 1:29) and Isaiah the prophet spoke of:

"He is despised and rejected by men, A Man of sorrows and acquainted with grief. And we hid, as it were, our faces from Him; He was despised, and we did not esteem Him."

— Isaiah 53:3 NKJV

The Coming Judgment!

Jesus then foretells the destruction of Jerusalem:

"For days will come upon you, when your enemies will set up a barricade around you... and they will not leave one stone

upon another in you, because you did not know the time of your visitation."

— Luke 19:43–44

This prophecy happened in AD70 when the Romans besieged Jerusalem and destroyed the temple—just as Jesus said. The phrase "not one stone will be left upon another" became reality, as Roman soldiers dismantled the temple stone by stone to extract melted gold from the fire.

This was not just history. It was judgment.

And Jesus did not rejoice in it—He wept over it!

A God Who Weeps:

Let this settle in your heart:

The God of heaven, the Creator of all things, weeps over those who reject Him. He does not delight in judgment. He grieves.

The weeping of Jesus over Jerusalem reveals:

- His long-suffering love for His people.
- His pain over spiritual blindness.
- His sorrow over judgment, even when it is just.

This is not a distant God. This is a Savior who feels, who laments, who pleads.

"How often I wanted to gather your children together, as a hen

gathers her chicks under her wings, but you were not willing!"

— Matthew 23:37

He came with open arms—but they would

The Righteous Anger of a Brokenhearted King:

After weeping over the city, Jesus did not turn away.

He continued forward—into the heart of Jerusalem, and straight to the temple.

Then He went into the temple and began to drive out those who bought and sold in it, saying to them, 'It is written, "My house is a house of prayer," but you have made it a den of thieves.'"

— Luke 19:45–46 NKJV

The Lord of the temple had returned—and He did not come quietly.

Jesus 'actions not by rage, but by righteous love. The word used for "drove out" in Greek is ἐξέβαλεν (exebalen)—meaning to cast out forcefully, but not recklessly. It is the same word used when Jesus cast out demons. This was holy cleansing, not emotional chaos.

What had become of the sacred place meant to welcome the nations and invite communion with God? It had become a marketplace. A place of profit. A place of corruption.

Jesus quoted from Isaiah 56:7, where God says, "My house shall be called a house of prayer for

all nations." But He followed it with Jeremiah 7:11, a strong rebuke:

"Has this house, which is called by My name, become a den of thieves in your eyes? Behold, I, even I, have seen it," says the Lord."

—Jeremiah 7:11 NKJV

They had defiled the temple, and Jesus—the true Temple—came to cleanse it.

A Piercing Prophetic Reality,

Pause and take this in:

- The Messiah rides in lowly and peaceful to fulfill Zechariah 9:9.
- He weeps with loud sobs over Jerusalem, mourning the fulfillment of Isaiah 53.
- He speaks words that precisely align with Daniel's timeline and predicts the destruction of the temple in Luke 19:44.
- Then He enters the temple, cleansing it just as Malachi prophesied:

""Behold, I send My messenger, and he will prepare the way before Me. And the Lord, whom you look for, Will suddenly come to His temple, Even the Messenger of the covenant, in whom you delight. Behold, He is coming," says the Lord of hosts. "But who can endure the day of His

coming? And who can stand when He appears? For He is like a refiner's fire and like launderers' soap."

— Malachi 3:1-2 NKJV

This was not just a moment in time—it was a culmination of centuries of prophecy.

The rejected King,

And yet, after all this… they still rejected Him.

Jesus remained in Jerusalem in the days that followed, teaching in the temple. The crowds were astonished. But the leaders enraged in jealousy over His popularity wanted Him dead.

This was the tragedy Jesus had already foreseen.

"He came to His own, and His own did not receive Him." John 1:11

And still, He stayed.

Still, He taught.

Still, He offered mercy.

This is love beyond understanding.

Closing Reflection: What Kind of King Do We Want?

Jesus did not come with a sword that day—He came with tears.

He did not ride into Jerusalem to take power—He came to give His life. He saw the very people who would shout "Crucify Him!"

And He wept—not for Himself, but for them.

Let this truth strike your heart:

The only place Jesus ever wept over in judgment was the city He came to save.

In this moment, the King stood between two mountains:

- Mount of Olives, where He wept,
- Mount Moriah, where He would be crucified.

And between them lies the temple, where worship was hollow, but hearts hardened.

Let us ask:

- Do we receive the King as He is—or only as we want Him to be?
- Do we allow Him to cleanse our hearts, or do we resist Him?
- Can we still feel the weight of His tears? May we not miss our day of visitation.

May we welcome the One who still comes—not in outward show, but in gentle truth, with eyes full of compassion and a heart ready to save.

Jesus quoted from Isaiah 56:7, where God says, "My house shall be called a house of prayer for all nations." But He followed it with Jeremiah 7:11, a strong rebuke:

"Has this house, which bears my Name, become a den of robbers to you? But I have been watching!"

Pause and take this in:

""Behold, I send My messenger, and he will prepare the way before Me. And the Lord, whom you seek, Will suddenly come to His temple, Even the Messenger of the covenant, in whom you delight. Behold, He is coming," says the Lord of hosts. "But who can endure the day of His coming? And who can stand when He appears? For He is like a refiner's fire and like launderers' soap."

— Malachi 3:1-2 NKJV

This was not just a moment in time—it was a culmination of centuries of prophecy.

"He came to His own, and His own did not receive Him."

— John 1:11

Jesus did not come with a sword that day—He came with tears.

He did not ride into Jerusalem to take power—He came to give His life. He saw the very people who would shout "Crucify Him!"

And He wept—not for Himself, but for them.

Let this truth strike your heart:

A Moment of Conviction and Invitation

Jesus wept over Jerusalem—not in anger, but in grief. He longed for them to recognize Him, to turn from empty religion and receive His peace. He still longs for that today. This is not just history—it is your moment of visitation. If you feel the weight of His love pressing on your heart…If you sense the gentle grief of a Savior who sees all and still loves…Do not turn away. This is your time to respond and to repent (to turn by renewing of your mind from your old fleshly ways). Let the King come into the temple of your heart—not to destroy, but to cleanse, to restore, and to dwell.

Prayer of Repentance and Salvation:

Lord Jesus,

I see Your tears.

I feel the weight of Your love.

You came for me. You wept for me. You died for me.

I confess that I have gone my own way. I have made room for many things of this world —but not for You.Today I open my heart. Come into my life, Lord.Cleans me. Forgive me.You are the Son of God who died and rose again. Be my Savior. Be my Lord.

I surrender all. In the name of Jesus. Amen.

CHAPTER FIVE: REJECTED BY HIS OWN BUT SOUGHT BY THE GREEKS

It was early the next morning—the 11th of Nisan, just four days before the Passover lamp would be slaughtered.

Jesus rose from Bethany once again and headed toward Jerusalem. As He walked with His disciples, something happened, that carried deep prophetic weight.

Now the next day, when they had come out from Bethany, He was hungry. And seeing from afar a fig tree having leaves, He went to see if perhaps He would find something on it. When He came to it, He found nothing but leaves, for it was not the season for figs. In response Jesus said to it, 'Let no one eat fruit from you ever again. 'And His disciples heard it."

— Mark 11:12–14 NKJV

This was not about a tree. This was about Israel—about the temple, and about every heart that bears the appearance of godliness but lacks true fruit.

Fig Leaves Without Fruit:

The fig tree had leaves, which suggested it should have fruit. But it did not. In the Old Testament, Israel is a symbol of a fig tree. (Jeremiah 24:1–10; Hosea 9:10). God had searched for fruit among His people for centuries. Now Jesus—God in the flesh—stood before a fig tree that symbolized the nation.

""I found Israel Like grapes in the wilderness; I saw your fathers as the firstfruits on the fig tree in its first season. But they went to Baal Peor And separated themselves to that shame; They became an abomination like the thing they loved."

— Hosea 9:10 NKJV

It was a visible sign of what He had already wept over:

Outward religion. Inward barrenness. Later that same day, Jesus entered the temple again—and began teaching.

He was not done cleansing the outer courts. He was about to confront the inner corruption.

The Authority of the King Challenged!

Jesus was met by religious leaders who demanded to know:

"By what authority are You doing these things? And who gave You this authority?"

— Mark 11:28

But He answered them with a question about John the Baptist—exposing their hypocrisy. They feared the people. They feared losing control. But they did not fear God.

Jesus followed with parables that pierced the heart:

- The Parable of the Two Sons (Matthew 21:28–32): One said "yes" but did not obey. The other said "no" but later repented.
- The Parable of the Wicked Tenants (Matthew 21:33–46): A clear reference to the religious leaders rejecting the prophets—and now rejecting the Son.
- The Parable of the Wedding Feast (Matthew 22:1–14): An open invitation to all, yet many rejected it. Those who came in without the right garments were cast out—showing that mere association is not enough. There must be true righteousness.

Prophecy Upon Prophecy

Every moment was drenched in fulfilled Scripture:

- The fig tree: A symbol of Jeremiah 8:13 "–There will be no figs on the tree, and their leaves will wither."
- The rejection of the Son: Fulfills Psalm 118:22 "–The stone the builders rejected has become the cornerstone."
- The warnings to the leaders: Point to Isaiah 5, the song of the vineyard that bore only wild grapes.

Jesus was not just speaking truth—He was fulfilling ancient prophecies with every word and step.

A Love That Warns

These were not cold theological debates. They were the cries of a rejected King, giving every opportunity for repentance. Though His tone was firm, His heart still bled.

The fig tree would wither. The temple would fall.

But the door of mercy was still open.

The Rejection and the Desire: Jews and Greeks in Contrast:

After Jesus had taught in the temple and confronted the religious leaders with authority and

compassion, something unexpected happened:

"Now there were certain Greeks among those who came up to worship at the feast. Then they came to Philip, who was from Bethsaida of Galilee, and asked him, saying, "Sir, we wish to see Jesus.""

— John 12:20-21 NKJV

This is no small detail. In the same temple where the religious leaders plotted to kill Him, Gentiles—outsiders—were drawn to Him.

It was a quiet yet thunderous moment:

The Jews, His own people, who had been given the covenants, the prophets, and the promises, were rejecting their Messiah—while the nations were beginning to come toward the Light.

A Prophetic Fulfillment Begins

This echoes the prophecy of Isaiah,

"Indeed He says, 'It is too small a thing that You should be My Servant To raise up the tribes of Jacob, And to restore the preserved ones of Israel; I will also give You as a light to the Gentiles, That You should be My salvation to the ends of the

earth.'""

— Isaiah 49:6 NKJV

Jesus knew what this meant. Their desire to see Him was a signal: The hour had come.

But Jesus answered them, saying, 'The hour has come that the Son of Man should be glorified.'"

— John 12:23 NKJV

Reflective Prayer & Invitation:

Lord Jesus,

You search not for leaves, but for fruit.

You are not impressed by outward forms, but by a humble, surrendered heart.

I confess—there are times I have had the appearance of devotion but lacked real obedience. Cleanse me again.

Search my heart. Remove all that is barren.

Let my life bear the fruit that pleases You: love, humility, obedience, and truth.

And if I'have never truly given You my life… I do so now. Come in. Be my Savior. Be my Lord.

I choose You—not in word only, but in truth. Forgive my sins. Make me new.

In the name of Jesus. Amen.

CHAPTER SIX: THE OLIVET DISCOURSE!

As the final days of Jesus' earthly ministry approached, the tension in Jerusalem was thick. The temple had just echoed with His rebuke of fruitless religion, and His heart had broken in weeping over the city that had rejected its Messiah. And now, as He left the temple for the last time, the shadow of the cross was already upon Him.

His disciples, unaware of how near the end was, drew His attention to the magnificent stones of the temple complex. But Jesus 'response pierced the illusion of permanence:

"Do you not see all these things? Assuredly, I say to you, not one stone shall be left here upon another, that shall not be thrown down."

—Matthew 24:2 NKJV

It was here, on the Mount of Olives overlooking Jerusalem, that Jesus sat and gave one of the most significant and sobering teachings in all of Scripture—a prophetic roadmap known as the Olivet Discourse. What followed was not only a foretelling of Jerusalem's fall, but a sweeping vision of the last days, the signs of His second coming, and the ultimate consummation of all things.

This chapter will walk through this monumental teaching, comparing the parallel accounts in Matthew 24, Mark 13, and Luke 21, while cross-referencing the book of Revelation and other

prophetic Scriptures. In this teaching, Jesus did not speak in parables—but in clear, urgent prophecy. These were not gentle warnings, but divine declarations meant to awaken every soul to watchfulness, repentance, and readiness. The same Jesus who wept over Jerusalem now calls us to discern the times, to endure through deception and tribulation, and to hold fast to the hope of His glorious return.

The Questions That Shaped the Discourse

The Olivet Discourse begins not with a statement, but with a question—or rather, multiple questions—asked by the disciples as they walked with Jesus from the temple to the Mount of Olives.

Matthew24:3 NKJV

Now as He sat on the Mount of Olives, the disciples came to Him privately, saying, 'Tell us, when will these things be? And what will be the sign of Your coming, and of the end of the age?'"

This account presents three distinct questions:

1. When will these things be? (referring to the destruction of the temple),
2. What will be the sign of Your coming?
3. And of the end of the age?

Matthew emphasizes the Messianic and eschatological hope of the disciples. They were not simply curious about the temple's fate—they wanted to know about His return and the end of time as they knew it. Their questions were prophetic in nature, revealing a hunger for the fulfillment of God's kingdom and justice.

But now contrast this with Luke 21:7 NKJV

"So, they asked Him, saying, 'Teacher, but when will these things be? And what sign will there be when these things are about to take place?'"

Luke's account focuses primarily on the immediate concern: the destruction of the temple and the signs that would precede it. This version appears more historical and practical, aimed at preparing believers for the coming siege of Jerusalem in 70 AD.

One Teacher, Two Layers of Prophecy

Both questions are valid—and Jesus answers both. But He does so by interweaving two timelines:

1. The near-term prophecy—fulfilled in 70 AD when the Roman armies besieged Jerusalem, destroyed the temple, and scattered the Jewish people.

2. The long-term prophecy—pointing to the final tribulation, the rise of false messiahs, the

abomination of desolation, and His second coming in glory.

Jesus' words in Matthew tend to emphasize the cosmic, end-time events, while Luke includes more details about the immediate signs leading to Jerusalem's fall. The Holy Spirit inspired the gospel writers to emphasize various aspects of the same teaching; each perfectly suited for their audience and purpose.

We now begin to walk through Jesus 'words—step by step—tracing how His answers unfold, how prophecy unfolds and how some of it still awaits its final fulfillment in the days ahead.

A Deeper Contrast: The Setting of the Questions:

Not only do Matthew and Luke record the disciples 'questions differently, but they also place them in different moments—and this distinction is more than just literary; it is deeply theological.

Luke's account: Luke 21:5-7 NKJV

"Then, as some spoke of the temple, how it was adorned with beautiful stones and donations, He said, 'These things which you see—the days will come in which not one stone shall be left upon another that shall not be thrown down. 'So, they asked Him, saying, 'Teacher, but when will these things be? And what sign will there be when these things are about to take place?'"

This conversation occurs within the temple courts. The disciples and onlookers are admiring the temple's grandeur—its gold, massive stones, and sacred offerings. Jesus then interrupts their admiration with a shocking prophecy of destruction. Here, the focus is immediate and practical: When will this temple be destroyed? The question flows naturally from the Lord's declaration. The audience seems larger, and the mood is public and sobering.

Matthew's account: Matthew 24:1-3 NKJV

"Then Jesus went out and departed from the temple, and His disciples came up to show Him the buildings of the temple. And Jesus said to them, 'Do you not see all these things?

Assuredly, I say to you, not one stone shall be left here upon another, that shall not be thrown down. 'Now as He sat on the Mount of Olives, the disciples came to Him privately, saying, 'Tell us, when will these things be? And what will be the sign of Your coming, and of the end of the age?'"

This is a private moment. Jesus has already left the temple—symbolically turning His back on the religious system that had rejected Him. As they cross the Kidron Valley and sit on the Mount of Olives, the disciples approach Him in private.

This setting is more intimate, contemplative, and eschatological. The disciples are not just asking about the destruction of buildings—they are asking about the end of the age, the coming of the Messiah, and the final fulfillment of God's plan.

Why this matters!

Understanding the difference in location and tone helps us grasp how the Lord was answering both a near-term and a long-term question. In the temple, His prophecy prepared believers for what was coming soon—the siege of Jerusalem, persecution, and tribulation. On the Mount of Olives, He lifted their eyes toward the final fulfillment, His second coming, and the eternal kingdom to come. Both audiences needed to hear the truth. One needed warning, the other needed watchfulness.

"Take Heed That No One Deceives You"

In both Matthew 24 and Luke 21, Jesus begins His answer not by giving specific dates or timelines, but by issuing a sobering spiritual warning:

— Matthew24:4 NKJV

"And Jesus answered and said to them: 'Take heed that no one deceives you. For many will come in My name, saying, "I am the Christ," and will deceive many.'"

— Luke 21:8 NKJV

"And He said: 'Take heed that you not be deceived. For many will come in My name, saying, "I am He," and, "The time has drawn near." Therefore, do not go after them.'"

This warning is the first sign Jesus gives—not wars, not earthquakes, not tribulation. The first sign of the end times is deception—especially religious deception.

It is important to note that in the original Greek, the word translated as "deceive" is πλανήσῃ (planēsē), meaning to lead astray, to cause to wander, to mislead. It implies more than just misinformation—it implies a seduction, a pulling away from the truth with something that sounds spiritual, even biblical.

A Prophetic Pattern of False Christs

In the decades and centuries following Jesus 'ascension, history records many false messiahs and self-proclaimed deliverers who led people into ruin. But Jesus' warning was not limited to those early years. The spirit of deception would increase as the end of the age draws near, and many would appear in His name—claiming divine authority, spiritual insight, and even prophetic gifts.

Paul echoes this in 2 Thessalonians 2:3–4, speaking of the man of lawlessness who will exalt himself as God in the temple. John warns of many antichrists already in the world (1 John 2:18). And Revelation tells us of the Beast and the False Prophet, performing signs to deceive the nations (Revelation 13).

The Call to Discernment and Watchfulness:

So, what is Jesus teaching us here? Before His disciples—or we—can understand the sequence of prophetic events, we must first understand the condition of our hearts. Prophecy is not just about timelines. It is about truth vs. lies, light vs. darkness, loyalty to Christ vs. seduction by the world. The very first posture Jesus calls us to is spiritual vigilance. Not fear, but faithfulness. Not sensationalism, but sobriety.

The Beginning of Sorrows

After warning of deception, Jesus continues:

— Matthew 24:6-8 NKJV

"And you will hear of wars and rumors of wars. See that you are not

troubled; for all these things must come to pass, but the end is not yet.

For nation will rise against nation, and kingdom against kingdom. And there will be famines, pestilences, and earthquakes in various places.

All these are the beginning of sorrows."

— Luke 21:9-11 NKJV

"But when you hear of wars and commotions, do not be terrified; for these things must come to pass first, but the end will not come immediately."

Then He said to them, "Nation will rise against nation, and kingdom against kingdom.

And there will be great earthquakes in various places, and famines and pestilences; and there will be fearful sights and great signs from heaven."

Prophetic Patterns: Near and Far Fulfillment

We must recognize that Jesus is speaking prophetically on two levels:

1. Near-Term Fulfillment: These signs would occur within the generation of the disciples. The Jewish-Roman wars (66–73 AD), the destruction of Jerusalem in 70 AD, earthquakes like the one in Laodicea (c. 60 AD), famines (Acts 11:28), and false messiahs all took place in the early church era.

2. End-Time Fulfillment: These signs will also intensify as we near the Second Coming. Revelation chapters 6–11 mirror many of these same signs: war, famine, plague, cosmic disturbances, and martyrdom. So, what Jesus describes is not merely a linear timeline but a cycle of contractions, like birth pains, growing closer and more intense as the end draws near. This is why He calls them "the beginning of sorrows" (Greek: ōdinōn — labor pains).

Persecution, Betrayal, and Endurance!

Next, Jesus shifts focus to the suffering of His followers:

Matthew 24:9-13

"Then they will deliver you up to tribulation and kill you, and you will be hated by all nations for My name's sake.

And then many will be offended, will betray one another, and will hate one another.

Then many false prophets will rise up and deceive many.

And because lawlessness will abound, the love of many will grow cold.

But he who endures to the end shall be saved."

— Luke 21:12-19 NKJV

"But before all these things, they will lay their hands on you and persecute you, delivering you up to the synagogues and prisons. You will be brought before kings and rulers for My name's sake. But it will turn out for you as an occasion for testimony. Therefore settle it in your hearts not to meditate beforehand on what you will answer; for I will give you a mouth and wisdom which all your adversaries will not be able to contradict or resist. You will be betrayed even by parents and brothers, relatives, and friends; and they will put some of you to death. "And you will be hated by all for My name's sack. But not a hair of your head shall be lost. By your patience possess your souls."

Faith Under Fire:

The warning here is not just about physical persecution—but also spiritual betrayal. The falling away of many. The rise of false prophets who twist truth for personal gain. The coldness of love as sin and selfishness increase.

But Jesus also gives hope: "He who endures to the end shall be saved." This is not a call to survive in our own strength but a call to abide in Christ, to remain faithful in the face of opposition.

Luke captures this beautifully with the phrase:

"By your patience, possess your souls."

The Gospel Will Be Preached to All Nations

Amid all the turmoil, Jesus assures us of something extraordinary:

— Matthew 24:14 NKJV

"And this gospel of the kingdom will be preached in all the world as a witness to all the nations, and then the end will come."

The darkness will grow, but the light will shine brighter. The gospel is not defeated by tribulation—it spreads because of it. Even in Revelation, the angel flying across the heavens proclaiming the "eternal gospel" (Revelation 14 :6).

The Abomination of Desolation: A Prophetic Signal

Matthew 24:15–16

"Therefore, when you see the 'abomination of desolation,' spoken of by Daniel the prophet, standing in the holy place" (whoever reads, let him understand),

then let those who are in Judea flee to the mountains."

— Luke 21:20–21

""But when you see Jerusalem surrounded by armies, then know that its desolation is near. Then let those who are in Judea flee to the mountains, let those who are in the midst of her depart, and let not those who are in the country enter her."

What Is the "Abomination of Desolation"?

The term comes from the book of Daniel (especially Daniel 9:27, 11:31, and 12:11). In the Hebrew, it refers to a sacrilegious defilement—something so spiritually offensive that it causes God's presence to withdraw and brings the wrath of God.

There are two levels of fulfillment:

1. Historical (Past) Fulfillment – 70 AD

Luke gives us clarity: "when you see Jerusalem surrounded by armies…" This occurred in 70 AD when the Roman general Titus besieged and destroyed Jerusalem.

- The Temple was destroyed
- Over one million Jews perished.
- Blood flowed through the streets of the Holy City

This was a judgment on the generation that rejected the Messiah (Matthew 23:37–38).

2. Prophetic (Future) Fulfillment – End Times

Matthew's wording, "standing in the holy place," hints at a future desecration of a restored Temple. Paul also speaks of this in 2 Thessalonians 2:3–4, where the man of sin (Antichrist) exalts himself as God in the Temple.

Likewise, in Revelation 13, the Beast demands worship and sets up an image—a global replay of Antiochus Epiphanes 'original blasphemy in 167 BC.

This will be the spark of the Great Tribulation.

A Time of Great Tribulation:

Matthew 24:21–22

"For then there will be great tribulation, such as has not been since the beginning of the world until this time, no, nor ever shall be.

And unless those days were shortened, no flesh would be saved; but for the elect's sake those days will be shortened."

Jesus describes a singular period of intense tribulation unlike anything in history—a time of:

- Global chaos
- Severe persecution
- Cosmic upheaval
- False messiahs and signs

This period echoes the judgments in Revelation 6–18, including:

- The opening of seals,
- Sounding of trumpets,
- Pouring out of bowls,
- And the rise of Babylon the Great.

Cosmic Signs and the Coming of the Son of Man

The discourse reaches its prophetic peak:

— Matthew 24:29–30

""Immediately after the tribulation of those days the sun will be darkened, and the moon will not give its light; the stars will fall from heaven, and the powers of the heavens will be shaken. Then the sign of

the Son of Man will appear in heaven, and then all the tribes of the earth will mourn, and they will see the Son of Man coming on the clouds of heaven with power and great glory."

This points us to Revelation 19—when Christ returns riding on a white horse, eyes like flames, crowned with many crowns, coming to judge and make war.

Luke's Pastoral Prophetic Warning Luke provides this soul-anchoring exhortation: Luke 21:34–36

""But take heed to yourselves, lest your hearts be weighed down with carousing, drunkenness, and cares of this life, and that Day come on you unexpectedly. For it will come as a snare on all those who dwell on the face of the whole earth. Watch therefore, and pray always that you may be counted worthy to escape all these things that will come to pass, and to stand before the Son of Man.""

Jesus was not just teaching prophecy to inform our minds—He was awakening hearts to prepare for His return.

Closing This Chapter with a Call to Watchfulness

The Olivet Discourse is not merely a timeline of events—it is a call to:

- Spiritual alertness
- Perseverance in holiness
- A heart anchored in eternal hope It is Jesus Himself who said,

"Heaven and earth will pass away, but My words will by no means pass away."

— Matthew 24:35

As we near the end of this chapter, let the weight of His words pierce through distractions and awaken a holy urgency. Whether we face persecution, deception, or delay—our eyes must stay on the returning King.

Reflective Prompt: Are You Ready?

The Lord Jesus has not spoken these words for us to speculate, but to awaken us.

- Are you living as though He could return at any moment?
- Have you allowed the cares of this life to dull your sensitivity to eternal things?
- Are you hiding in religion like the Pharisees, or have you truly surrendered your heart to the Lord of glory?

The warning is not just for the unbelieving world—it is also for those who claim His name yet have grown spiritually cold. Let this moment be a turning point.

Closing Prayer:

Lord Jesus, Son of the Living God, You warned us not to be unaware.

You wept over a city that did not know its hour of visitation.

Today, I ask You to awaken my heart.

Strip away my pride, my distractions, my delay.

Forgive me for the times I have lived as if this world is all there is. Set my heart on fire with watchfulness.

Prepare me for the day of Your return.

If I have not yet surrendered to You, Jesus,

I do so now—fully, completely. Be my Savior, be my Lord. Come and rule in my life.

And until the day I see You face to face,

keep me faithful, burning with holy expectation. In Your mighty and precious name,

Amen.

"Even so, come, Lord Jesus." (Revelation 22 :20

CHAPTER SEVEN: WHEN THE FIG TREE BUDS

As Jesus concluded His prophetic discourse on the Mount of Olives, He turned to His disciples with a command not wrapped in mystery but in clarity:

"Now learn this parable from the fig tree..." (Matthew 24:32).

This was not a vague illustration—this was a living parable, unfolding in their very presence. Jesus often taught with metaphors and agricultural imagery, but this moment was different. The fig tree was not just a random plant—it was a national symbol of Israel, and the budding of that fig tree was a sign, both literal and prophetic of something far greater.

"When its branch has already become tender and puts forth leaves, you know that summer is near.

So, you also when you see all these things, know that it is near—at the doors!"

— (Matthew 24:32–33)

This was not a call to guess the day or hour—Jesus had made that clear. Instead, it was a command to watch the signs. Just as the leaves of a fig tree reveal the change of season, so the unfolding events around us are revealing the nearness of the return of the Son of Man.But this parable is more than just symbolic. The fig tree budded again in history—the nation of Israel, scattered and lifeless for two millennia, became a nation once more in 1948. It is as if the once barren fig tree began to sprout its leaves, just as Jesus said it would. We are not waiting for the fig tree to bud. It already has. And this changes everything. It places us squarely within the generation that must stay awake, stay alert, and discern the times. To ignore this would be to repeat the very blindness Jesus wept over in Jerusalem.

The Budding Fig Tree: More Than a Symbol!

In Matthew 24:32–35, Jesus speaks clearly:

"Now learn this parable from the fig tree: When its branch has already become tender and puts forth leaves, you know that summer is near.

So, you also when you see all these things, know that it is near—

at the doors!"

And in Luke 21:29–31, He adds a layer:

"Look at the fig tree, and all the trees. When they are already budding, you see and know for yourselves that summer is now near.

So, you also, when you see these things happening, know that

the kingdom of God is near."

Jesus is drawing from the natural world to explain spiritual reality. In the same way we watch the seasons change by seeing the trees, He commands us to watch the world, the signs, the nations (all the trees), and especially Israeli —the prophetic fig tree of Scripture.

Why the Fig Tree Represents Israel:

Throughout the Old Testament, Israel is a symbol of the fig tree:

- Hosea 9:10 "–I found Israel like grapes in the wilderness; I saw your fathers as the firstfruits on the fig tree…"
- Jeremiah 24 – The prophet shown two baskets of figs, representing the people of Judah—some good, some bad.
- Micah 7:1 – The prophet laments the absence of "first-ripe figs," symbolizing Israel's spiritual barrenness.

Even earlier in Jesus 'ministry, He had cursed a fig tree that bore no fruit (Mark 11:12–14), a powerful image of Israel's spiritual condition at the time—outwardly religious, but inwardly barren.So when Jesus speaks of the fig tree budding, He is signaling that Israel, once seemingly dead and scattered, will come alive again. And we see this happening right in our eyes, not only are the diaspora Jews coming back to Israel, but Israel is at its most prosperity. indeed, the fig tree (Israel) is budding and all the national a sign of prosperity for the entire world This is that generation the Lord Jesus Christ prophesied of. These are the things the prophets of old searched the scriptures but could not understand. We are that generation that shall see it all, the signs of the end of the age are everywhere. Wars and rumors wars are in the news; it is a sensitive time we are living in anything can happen at anytime.

Prophecy Fulfilled in Our Generation:

For 2,000 years, Israel did not exist as a nation. But in May 1948, against all odds, Israel was reborn. A nation that had been dormant suddenly blossomed.

The fig tree budded.

And Jesus said, "when you see these things…"—not "if"— "you know the Kingdom is near." This was not just a political or historical event. It was prophetic fulfillment. Jesus told us in advance, and now we are seeing it in real time.

"Assuredly, I say to you, this generation will by no means pass away till all these things take place." (Matthew 24:34)

We are that generation. We are not waiting for the signs—they are unfolding. We are not waiting for the fig tree to bud—it has already happened. We are not in the season of waiting for the King; we are in the season of preparing for His return.

Watchfulness in a World of Wars

Jesus went on to say:

"And you will hear of wars and rumors of wars. See that you are not troubled; for all these things must come to pass, but the end is not yet."

— Matthew 24:6 NKJV

We live in an hour when rumors of wars have become headlines. Global conflict looms constantly—whether in Eastern Europe, the Middle East, Asia, or Africa. Military powers posture. Nations threaten. Peace feels fragile. And yet Jesus told us not to panic—but to be watchful.

He did not tell us to speculate. He told us to prepare.

"Take heed, watch and pray; for you do not know when the time is."

—Mark 13:33 NKJV

Watchfulness is not fear—its faith awake. It is the posture of a bride who knows her Bridegroom could appear at any moment.

The Parable Actually Happened

What makes this parable even more stunning is that Jesus acted it out during His final week. He approached a fig tree looking for fruit, and when He found none, He cursed it. The tree withered by the next day (Matthew 21:18–19; Mark 11:12–14, 20–21).

This was not just about a tree—it was about a generation that had the appearance of life but no fruit of repentance. And that same warning echoes today.

Many claim to follow Jesus, but their lives bear no fruit. Many know the form of godliness but deny its power. The warning is not just to Israel then—it is to the Church now.

Final Call: A Generation at the Door

We are that generation.

We are watching prophecy fulfilled in real time. The fig tree has budded.

Wars and rumors of wars at the doorstep. Knowledge has increased (lawlessness). Israel is surrounded by enemy countries. Nations are aligning as foretold.

Hearts are growing cold.

Yet the Gospel is still being preached to all nations.

This is the hour to wake up!

"And what I say to you, I say to all: Watch!"

—Mark 13:37

A Call to Reflect and Respond

If you' are spiritually distracted, busy, or asleep—now is the time to realign. If fear of world events has gripped, you—let Jesus anchor your heart.

If you' have never surrendered your life to Christ—do not wait another moment.

Pray with me:

Father, open my eyes to the times I am living in. I see the signs. I hear the warnings. I want to be ready. Forgive me for my spiritual slumber and any compromise in my heart. Fill me with Your Spirit. Help me to live watchfully, faithfully, and fruitfully in this hour. I receive You as my Savior, and I surrender to You as my Lord. Make me ready for Your return. In Jesus 'name. Amen.

A Call to Watchfulness: The Parables that Follow

Immediately after teaching the parable of the fig tree, Jesus gives three striking parables—each carrying the weight of urgency, responsibility, and eternal consequence. They are not random stories. They are prophetic instructions for the generation that sees the fig tree bud—our generation.

1. The Faithful and Evil Servants

Jesus contrasts two types of servants—one who is faithful and watching, and one who delays and becomes careless.

"Assuredly, I say to you that he will make him ruler over all his goods. and begins to beat his fellow servants, and to eat and drink with the drunkards, the master of that servant will come on a day when he is not looking for him and at an hour that he is not aware of, and will cut him in two and appoint him his portion with the hypocrites. There shall be weeping and gnashing of teeth."

— Matthew 24:47, 49-51 NKJV

Contrast with Luke 12:42–48:

"And the Lord said, "Who then is that faithful and wise steward, whom his master will make ruler over his household, to give them their portion of food in due season? Blessed is that servant whom his master will find so doing when he comes. Truly, I say to you that he will make him ruler over all that he has. But if that servant says in his heart, 'My master is delaying his coming,' and begins to beat the male and female servants, and to eat and drink and be drunk, the master of that servant will come

on a day when he is not looking for him, and at an hour when he is not aware, and will cut him in two and appoint him his portion with the unbelievers. And that servant who knew his master's will, and did not prepare himself or do according to his will, shall be beaten with many stripes. But he who did not know, yet committed things deserving of stripes, shall be beaten with few. For everyone to whom much is given, from him much will be required; and to whom much has been committed, of him they will ask the more."

— Luke 12:42-48 NKJV

Luke's account emphasizes responsibility: "To whom much is given, much will be required."

The warning here is not to grow spiritually lazy. If we know Christ is returning soon, how should that affect our daily lives, our priorities, our devotion?

2. The Wise and Foolish Virgins:

""“Then the kingdom of heaven shall be likened to ten virgins who took their lamps and went out to meet the bridegroom. Now five of them were wise, and five were foolish. Those who were foolish took their lamps and took no oil with them, but the wise took oil in their vessels with their lamps. But while the bridegroom was delayed, they all slumbered and slept. "And at midnight a cry was heard: 'Behold, the bridegroom is coming; go out to meet him!' Then all those virgins arose and trimmed their lamps. And the foolish said to the wise, 'Give us some of your oil, for our lamps are going out.' But the wise answered, saying, 'No, lest there should not be enough for us and you; but go rather to those who sell, and buy for yourselves.' And while they went to buy, the bridegroom came, and those who were ready went in with him to the wedding; and the door was shut. "Afterward the other virgins came also, saying, 'Lord, Lord, open to us!' But he answered and said, 'Assuredly, I say to you, I do not know you.' "Watch therefore, for you know neither the day nor the hour in which the Son of Man is coming."

Matthew 25:1-13 NKJV

This parable focuses not on servants, but on believers—those expecting the Bridegroom. All ten are waiting, all fall asleep, but only five have enough oil when He comes.

"And the door was shut' ... Lord, Lord, open to us! 'But He answered' ... I do not know you.'" (vv. 10–12)

This is a wake-up call to the Church. Oil often represents the Holy Spirit—intimacy with God. Many profess Christ, but only those whose lives are full of His presence will be ready when He returns.

Contrast with Revelation 3:15–20 (Church of Laodicea):

" "I know your works, that you are neither cold nor hot. I could wish you were cold or hot. So then, because you are lukewarm, and neither cold nor hot, I will vomit you out of My mouth. Because you say, 'I am rich, have become wealthy, and have need of nothing'—and do not know that you are wretched, miserable, poor, blind, and naked— I counsel you to buy from Me gold refined in the fire, that you may be rich; and white garments, that you may be clothed, that the shame of your nakedness may not be revealed; and anoint your eyes with eye salve, that you may see. As many as I love, I rebuke and chasten. Therefore, be zealous and repent. Behold, I stand at the door and knock. If anyone hears My voice and opens the door, I will come in to him and dine with him, and he with Me."

— Revelation 3:15-20 NKJV

They thought they were rich, but Jesus called them lukewarm and blind. He stood outside the door, knocking. Just like the bridegroom in the parable.

3. The Parable of the Talents

Matthew 25:14–30

Here Jesus speaks not of watching or waiting, but of working. Each servant is entrusted with resources. Two invest and multiply, but one hides his talent in fear and laziness.

"Well done, good and faithful servant... Enter into the joy of your lord." (v. 21)

"You wicked and lazy servant... Cast the unprofitable servant into outer darkness." (vv. 26, 30)

Cross-reference with Luke 19:11–27 – Parable of the Minas:

Though similar, this version is told before Jesus enters Jerusalem. It adds another dimension—a

noble goes to receive a kingdom, but his citizens reject him. Jesus is clearly pointing to Himself.

The Urgency of Our Time:

Each parable follows the fig tree for a reason. Jesus knew that when Israel would bud again, when the signs would begin to unfold, His people would need clarity:

- Watchfulness is not optional—it is a command.
- Readiness is not emotional—it is spiritual preparation.
- Fruitfulness is not extra—it is expected. This is

not the time to be asleep.

This is not the time to be lukewarm.

This is not the time to hide what God has given you.

"He who has an ear, let him hear what the Spirit says to the churches."

— (Revelation 2–3)

Final Reflection: The Tree Has Budded—What Will You Do?

The fig tree has budded.

Jerusalem has returned to Jewish hands.

The signs Jesus warned about are not in the distant future—they are unfolding before our eyes. The generation that sees these things will not pass away until all is fulfilled (Matthew 24:34). The questions now shift from "What time is it?" to "What will you do with this time?"

Will you be like the servant who stayed faithful even when it seemed the Master delayed?

Or like the one who said in his heart, "He won't come yet," and began to drift? Will you be found with oil in your lamp, burning with holy expectation?

Or knocking on the door too late, saying "Lord, Lord," only to hear Him say, "I never knew you"?

God is not asking for your perfection.

He is inviting you into repentance.

He is not waiting for your performance. He wants your surrender.

This is a call to awaken—to open your eyes to the hour and your heart to the Lord of the harvest.

A Call to Prayer and Repentance:

If you are a believer, but you have been spiritually asleep come back to your First Love.

If you'have been hiding your "talent," wasting time or gifts—ask the

Lord to reignite your purpose.

If you'have been lukewarm—ask Him to set your heart ablaze again.

And if you have never truly received Jesus Christ as your Lord and Savior, this is the moment. Do not delay. This is the time. He is calling.

Pray with me:

Father God, I recognize the hour I am living in. I see the signs all around me, and I hear Your voice calling me. I repent—for my sins, for my distance, for my delay. Forgive me. Wash me. Make me new. Fill me with the oil of Your Holy Spirit. Teach me to watch, to wait, and to work while it is still day. I surrender all. Be my Savior, my Lord, my Master, and my King. I want to be ready when You return. In Your holy name Jesus, I pray. Amen.

CHAPTER EIGHT: WHAT WILL BE THE SIGNS?

DISCERNING THE COMING OF THE LORD AND THE END OF THE AGE

The disciples came to Jesus with an urgent and intimate question—one that has echoed through every generation since:

"Tell us, when will these things be? And what will be the sign of Your coming, and of the end of the age?"

—Matthew 24:3 NKJV

This question—asked privately on the Mount of Olives—reveals the hunger of the disciples to understand the future. They were not just asking about the destruction of the temple, but about Jesus "'coming" and the "end of the age."

To understand the Lord's answer, we must first understand the Greek words used:

- “Coming” – παρουσία (parousia):

Not just an arrival, but an ongoing presence or revealing. It refers to the visible return of

Christ with power and glory—His second coming, not merely a spiritual visitation.

- “End” – συντέλεια (synteleia):

Not merely the termination of something, but the climactic consummation—the final wrapping up of an age with judgment and transition into the next.

A Contrast of Accounts: Matthew 24 vs. Luke 21

Though both chapters report the same general teaching of Jesus, they hold different emphases:

- Luke 21 includes more near-term fulfillment, such as the destruction of Jerusalem in AD 70.
- Matthew 24 looks further into the future, with signs leading up to the Great Tribulation and the second coming of Christ.

For example:

In Luke 21:20, Jesus says:

“But when you see Jerusalem surrounded by armies, then

know that its desolation is near.”

This was fulfilled historically in 70 AD

But in Matthew 24:15, Jesus says:

“Therefore when you see the ‘abomination of desolation,’

spoken of by Daniel the prophet, standing in the holy

place..."

This points to a future desecration, tied to end-times prophecy in Daniel 9 and the rise of the Antichrist.

Signs of the Coming King:

Jesus outlined straightforward signs that would characterize the end of the age. Let us list and

reflect on these with cross-references:

1. Deception (Matthew 24:4–5)

"Many will come in My name... and will deceive many." Compare: 1 Timothy 4:1 "–Some will depart from the faith, giving heed to deceiving spirits.

2. Wars and rumors of wars (Matthew 24:6)

These are birth pains, not the end—but signs that the world is groaning.

Compare: Revelation 6 :3–4 – The red horse of war.

3. Famines, pestilences, earthquakes (Matthew 24:7; Luke 21:11)

These multiply today—earthquakes in strange places, pandemics, food crises. Compare: Revelation 6 :5–8 – The black and pale horses of famine and death.

4. Persecution of believers (Matthew 24:9)

"You will be hated by all nations for My name's sake." Compare: Revelation 6 :9–11 – The cry of the martyrs.

5. Lawlessness and cold love (Matthew 24:12) The collapse of truth and morality breeds chaos.

Compare: 2 Thessalonians 2 :3 "–The man of lawlessness..."

6. The Gospel preached to all nations (Matthew 24:14)

Before the end comes, Jesus said the Gospel must go global.

Compare: Revelation 14 :6 – The angel with the eternal gospel flying across the heavens.

Watching the World Through Prophetic Eyes

As we examine these signs today, they are no longer distant echoes—they are present realities. What Jesus described is unfolding before our very eyes:

- Global instability.
- Moral confusion.
- Religious deception.
- Technological control.
- Israel back in the land.
- The Gospel penetrating every people group.

These signs are converging—not sequentially, but simultaneously, like labor pains before birth.

Jesus said:

"Now when these things begin to happen, look up and lift up your heads, because your redemption draws near."

—Luke 21:28

The Urgency of Watchfulness:

The Lord did not give us these signs to stir speculation—but to awaken readiness. He spoke clearly:

"Take heed, watch and pray; for you do not know when the time is."

—Mark 13:33 NKJV

And again:

"But of that day and hour no one knows, not even the angels of heaven, but My Father only."

—Matthew 24:36 NKJV

Yet, while the exact hour is unknown, the season is knowable. Just as a fig tree's budding shows summer is near, so these prophetic events signal that His coming is near—at the door.

"So, you also, when you see all these things, know that it is near—at the doors!"

—Matthew 24:33 NKJV

A World on Edge—Echoes of Prophecy Today

Every news headline, every global tremor, every war, and crisis are whispering: He is coming.

- Artificial intelligence and global digital systems suggest the infrastructure for Revelation 13's mark of the beast.
- Peace treaties and unrest in Israel reflect 1 Thessalonians 5 :3 "–When they say, 'Peace and safety! 'Then sudden destruction comes upon them."
- Global religious unity movements echo Revelation 17's false religious system—Babylon the Great.

The world is preparing for a false peace, a false savior, and a final judgment—but the Church must prepare for the true King.

A Piercing Warning:

Jesus followed His prophecy with stories—parables—to pierce the heart and drive home a single point:

Be ready. Be watchful. Be faithful.

He spoke of:

- A faithful servant vs. a lazy servant (Matthew 24:45–51)
- Wise virgins vs. foolish virgins (Matthew 25:1–13)
- Stewards with talents (Matthew 25:14–30)

In all of them, the question is the same:

Will you be found ready, serving, and believing when He returns?

"Watch therefore, for you do not know what hour your Lord is coming."

—Matthew 24:42 NKJV

A Call to the Heart

If you are already a follower of Christ, these words are a wake-up call. Now is not the time for lukewarm Christianity, for compromise or spiritual slumber. Now is the time to repent, rekindle your fire, and stand faithful.

But if you are not yet born again, or if you are unsure, hear the voice of Jesus Himself:

"Behold, I stand at the door and knock. If anyone hears My voice and opens the door, I will come in..."

—Revelation 3 :20 NKJV

He is not only coming for the world—He is coming for you. He died for your sins, rose again for your justification, and will return as King and Judge. Will you be ready?

Reflective Prayer:

Lord Jesus,

You warned us in love so that we would not be caught off guard.

You told us what the signs would look like,

so that we would lift our heads and not harden our hearts. I repent, Lord, of every way I'have grown cold.

Every moment I'have loved the world more than You. I open my heart to You.

I want to be ready—not only to escape judgment, but to see You face to face and hear,

"Well done, good and faithful servant."

CHAPTER 9: A SILENT DAY, A TREACHEROUS PLOT

By now we are at the 13th of Nisan, just one day before the Passover celebration in Jerusalem. Unlike the previous days, which are marked by intense public teaching, prophetic warnings, and emotional confrontations, this day appears silent in the Gospel records. Jesus is no longer in the temple courts or confronting the religious leaders. The noise dies down. The crowd's shouts of "Hosanna" have faded. It is in this stillness that the darkest plot begins to take shape.

Though the Gospels record little of Jesus 'public activity on this day, heaven and hell were both at work. In the quiet shadows, the religious leaders conspired to put Jesus to death, and a willing accomplice stepped forward—Judas Iscariot.

"Then one of the twelve, called Judas Iscariot, went to the chief priests, and said, 'What are you willing to give me if I deliver Him to you? 'And they counted out to him thirty pieces of silver. So, from that time he sought opportunity to betray Him."

—Matthew 26:14–16 NKJV

This betrayal did not take Jesus by surprise. He had long known what was coming, even naming Judas at the Last Supper. Yet what's striking is the prophetic precision of it all. Even the amount of silver—thirty pieces—was foretold by the prophet Zechariah:

"So, they weighed out for my wages thirty pieces of silver. And the Lord said to me, 'Throw it to the potter'—that princely price they set on me."

—Zechariah 11:12–13

Judas 'betrayal was not merely an act of greed or bitterness—it was the fulfillment of divine prophecy, woven into God's redemptive plan.

Though Judas walked with Jesus for over three years—seeing His miracles, hearing His teachings, and even partaking in ministry—his heart remained untouched by true devotion. His betrayal reveals a sobering truth: proximity to Christ is different from loyalty to Christ.

Scripture does not give us a detailed psychological profile of Judas, but it gives us enough to discern his downward spiral. In John 12:6, we learn that Judas was a thief, keeping the money

bag and helping himself to what was in it. His outward concern for the poor masked a heart consumed with greed. But greed alone was not the whole story.

"Then Satan entered Judas, surnamed Iscariot, who was numbered among the twelve."

—Luke 22:3

This chilling statement marks a turning point. Judas opened a door in his heart long before Satan entered. Through selfish ambition, secret sin, and a hardened will, he created the space for Satan to gain a foothold.

Judas, like many Jews, may have expected a political Messiah—a revolutionary who would overthrow Rome. As time passed and it became clear that Jesus 'kingdom was not of this world, disillusionment could have settled in. When Jesus spoke of His impending death rather than national victory, Judas began to see Him as a failed messiah—or worse, an opportunity wasted.

Still, the most tragic aspect of Judas 'betrayal is not just the act—it is his closeness to Christ at the time of his fall. In the Garden, he would betray the Son of God with a kiss.

"But Jesus said to him, 'Judas, are you betraying the Son of Man with a kiss?'"

—Luke 22:48

The kiss, in Jewish culture, was a sign of honor, intimacy, and respect—used by disciples to greet their teachers. That Judas used this very gesture as the sign of betrayal reveals the depth of his deception and the sorrow in Jesus 'response.

This moment, too, was foretold.

"Even my own familiar friend in whom I trusted, who ate my bread, has lifted up his heel against me."

—Psalm 41:9 NKJV

Now we come to a pivotal moment in the timeline of the Lord's final days. The Gospel writers clearly say that this was two days before the Passover—an important prophetic marker as the Lamb of God prepared to offer Himself for the sin of the world.

"After two days it was the Passover and the Feast of Unleavened Bread. And the chief priests and the scribes sought how they might take Him by trickery and put Him to death."

—Mark 14:1 NKJV

"Now it came to pass, when Jesus had finished all these sayings, that He said to His disciples, 'You know that after two days is the Passover, and the Son of Man will be delivered up to be crucified.'"

—Matthew 26:1–2 NKJV

The timing is deliberate and divine. The Passover, a feast commemorating the deliverance of Israel from Egypt through the blood of the lamb, now found its fulfillment in the One to whom it had always pointed. Jesus Himself confirms the countdown: "after two days," the true Passover Lamb would be delivered up.

This declaration was not just a prediction—it was a prophetic alignment with God's eternal calendar. The Lamb had to be slain at the appointed time (Exodus 12:6). As Jewish families prepared to sacrifice their lambs on the 14th of Nisan, the sinless Son of God was preparing to lay down His life at the exact hour. But as Jesus revealed this to His disciples, something else was unfolding in secret: the plot to betray Him was already in motion.The chief priests and scribes, blinded by jealousy and religious pride, were seeking a way to arrest Him—not during the feast, they said, lest there be an uproar among the people (Matthew 26:5). Ironically, despite their scheming, Jesus would be crucified precisely during the feast. Not because of their plans, but in fulfillment of God's sovereign will.

"Him, being delivered by the determined purpose and foreknowledge of God, you have taken by lawless hands, have crucified, and put to death."

—Acts 2:23 (NKJV)

This moment pierces the heart with two contrasts: Jesus, knowingly walking toward the cross in obedience to the Father—and the religious elite, plotting in darkness to destroy the Light of the world. It is here, between divine obedience and human rebellion, that the soul must choose its response.

This was the 12th of Nisan, and Jewish families were preparing for the sacred feast. But in the village of Bethany, something far more sacred was happening: a woman anointed the body of Christ for burial. This anointing took place in the house of Simon the leper, a man once outcast by disease, now hosting the Lord of glory at his table.

"And being in Bethany at the house of Simon the leper, as He sat at the table, a woman came having an alabaster flask of very costly oil of spikenard. Then she broke the flask and poured it on His head."

—Mark 14:3 NKJV

"A woman came to Him having an alabaster flask of very costly fragrant oil, and she poured it on His head as He sat at the table."

—Matthew 26:7 NKJV

This was not Mary of Bethany, who anointed His feet days earlier (John 12), but another unnamed woman, moved by the Spirit, stepping into the divine mystery unfolding. She broke the flask and poured the oil—not sparingly, but fully—on His head, marking Him as the true Anointed One. The word Christos means Anointed One—and here, for burial, He was truly and prophetically anointed. The room was filled with the fragrance of worship. But not all received the moment rightly.

"But when His disciples saw it, they were indignant, saying, 'Why this waste? For this fragrant oil might have been sold for much and given to the poor.'"

—Matthew 26:8–9 NKJV

"But Jesus said, 'Let her alone. Why do you trouble her? She has done an efficient work for Me... She has come beforehand to anoint My body for burial. Assuredly, I say to you, wherever this gospel is preached in the whole world, what this woman has done will also be told as a memorial to her.'"

—Mark 14:6, 8–9 NKJV

Here we see two responses again: one of love, sacrifice, and prophetic recognition… and another of criticism, calculation, and blindness. While others argued about the cost, this woman saw the value of Jesus. She understood what even the disciples struggled to grasp—that He was going to die, and this moment was part of His preparation. This event sets the tone for what follows: the betrayal of Judas, the final Passover, and the cross itself. As the religious leaders' plot and Judas prepares to betray, a woman worships. And Jesus honors her act for all eternity. This is not just history—it is an invitation. As the clock of prophecy ticks toward the crucifixion, we must ask ourselves: will we criticize the cost of devotion, or will we pour it all out at His feet?

A Call to the Heart:

As the alabaster flask was broken and poured out, so too would the body of Christ be broken and His blood poured out for the sins of the world. In that quiet home in Bethany, long before the crowds would shout "Crucify Him," one woman understood what even the closest disciples missed: Jesus came to die.

The question that remains is this—what will you do with this Jesus?

Will you hold back, calculating the cost? Or will you give Him everything, no matter the opinions of others? The oil she poured was costly, but it could not compare to the value of the One she anointed. Her act was an offering of worship, love, and prophetic surrender—and it still speaks today. Wherever the gospel is preached, her story follows, not because she was famous, but because she recognized Him.

Do you recognize Him today?

A Prayer of Surrender:

Lord Jesus,

You are the Anointed One, the Lamb of God, the King of glory who came not to be served, but to give Your life as a ransom for many.

Today, like the woman who poured out the oil, I come with all that I am. I pour out my pride, my sin, my past, my future.

I break the flask of my own control and lay it at Your feet. Forgive me, cleanse me, and anoint me with Your Spirit.

If I have known about You but not truly known You,

I open my heart now to receive You as Savior and Lord.

You died for my sins and rose again, and I confess that You are the Son of God. Let my life be a memorial of worship, oh Lord

A fragrance pleasing to You in the Holy name of Jesus, Amen.

Chapter 10: The Price of Betrayal and the Preparation of the Passover

It was now the fourteenth day of Nisan—the day of preparation, also known as the first day of Unleavened Bread. The final countdown to the cross had begun. On this day, while the city was bustling with preparations for the Passover lambs to be slain, a much darker preparation was quietly unfolding: the betrayal of the Lamb of God.

"Then one of the twelve, called Judas Iscariot, went to the chief priests, and said, 'What are you willing to give me if I deliver Him to you? 'And they counted out to him thirty pieces of silver. So, from that time he sought opportunity to betray Him."

—Matthew 26:14–16 (NKJV)

This act of betrayal was no surprise to the Lord. It was the fulfillment of ancient prophecy. Zechariah had written centuries earlier:

"So, they weighed out for my wages thirty pieces of silver. And the Lord said to me, 'Throw it to the potter'—that princely price they set on Me."

—Zechariah 11:12–13

The same price paid for a common slave (Exodus 21:32) was now offered for the Son of God. This moment marks a sharp descent toward Golgotha—a collision of divine sovereignty and human rebellion. Judas, one of the twelve, one who had seen the miracles and heard the

teachings, had now made his decision. And it was on this same day, while the disciples were asking Jesus where they should prepare the Passover meal, that betrayal was already in motion.

Mark's gospel records:

"After two days it was the Passover and the Feast of Unleavened Bread. And the chief priests and the scribes sought how they might take Him by trickery and put Him to death."

—Mark 14:1

And again:

"Now on the first day of Unleavened Bread, when they killed the Passover lamb, His disciples said to Him, 'Where do You want us to go and prepare, that You may eat the Passover?'"

—Mark 14:12

What the disciples did not yet see was that the true Passover Lamb was already present among them. As they prepared the table, Heaven was preparing the cross.

Before we enter the Upper Room, we pause to remember betrayal, though evil, was woven into the redemptive plan of God. The price of our salvation would be paid in full—not in silver, but in blood.

The Spiritual Conflict Behind the Betrayal

Judas did not act in isolation. While his heart had long been drifting from the Lord—covetous, critical, and hardened—the Scriptures make it clear that something deeper was at play. His betrayal was not merely a political miscalculation or personal offense; it was the climax of a spiritual battle.

"Then Satan entered Judas, surnamed Iscariot, who was numbered among the twelve."

—Luke 22:3 NKJV

This verse reveals what had been brewing in the unseen realm. The adversary, Satan, who had looked for from the beginning to destroy the seed of the woman (Genesis 3:15), now found a willing vessel. Judas opened the door through greed and unresolved darkness in his heart. And once that door opened, the enemy entered.

It is crucial to understand this was not possession against Judas 'will—it was agreement. Judas had heard every teaching of Christ, seen the miracles, saw the raising of the dead, and yet, his heart never fully surrendered. He followed but did not believe. He listened but did not repent. He was among the twelve, but not truly of the twelve.

John's Gospel pulls back the curtain further:

"The devil having already put it into the heart of Judas Iscariot, Simon's son, to betray Him..."

—John 13:2 NKJV

This was not a sudden act of impulse. It was a slow descent—one that began when Judas began stealing from the money box (John 12:6). One compromise led to another. His love of money had opened the door to deception, just as the Scriptures warn:

"For the love of money is a root of all kinds of evil, for which some

have strayed from the faith in their greediness and pierced themselves through with many sorrows."

—1 Timothy 6:10 (NKJV)

Judas greediness for money becomes an open door for satan —he became an instrument of darkness. And yet, even in this, God's sovereign plan of redemption had to unfold. The betrayal would not end the ministry of Jesus; it would start the moment of greatest glory—the cross.

Here we find the tension of the Gospel: divine sovereignty and human responsibility. Judas was not a puppet. He chose betrayal. But God, in His wisdom, used even that betrayal to fulfill prophecy and secure salvation.

"Even My own familiar friend in whom I trusted, who ate My bread, has lifted up his heel against Me."

—Psalm 41:9

Jesus quoted this in John 13:18 to show that this betrayal was foretold. It was necessary. The Lamb of God had to be handed over. The Son of God had to be lifted up.

And so, the spiritual conflict intensifies. While the disciples prepared for a feast, the enemy prepared for a strike. But in the wisdom of God, what Satan meant for destruction would become the very means of our deliverance.

The Upper Room: Covenant, Conflict, and Communion:

As the day of Unleavened Bread arrived, the disciples asked Jesus where He wanted them to prepare the Passover meal. His reply was prophetic and precise:

"Go into the city to a certain man, and say to him, 'The Teacher says, "My time is at hand; I will keep the Passover at your house with My disciples."'"

—Matthew 26:18 NKJV

This was not a last-minute arrangement. It was a divine appointment. Every detail of this meal was orchestrated by the sovereign hand of God. The Lamb of God would celebrate the feast that pointed to His own sacrifice—with His disciples—on the exact day God had ordained. As they reclined together, Jesus dropped a devastating revelation:

"Assuredly, I say to you, one of you will betray Me."

—Matthew 26:21

A hush must have filled the room. Each disciple, struck with the awareness of their own frailty, asked, "Lord, is it I?" This moment revealed not just the traitor—but the weakness of all. Even the most loyal could fail. Judas, too, asked the question. But Jesus 'answer was more piercing:

"You have said it."

—Matthew 26:25

Even in this moment of betrayal, Jesus did not expose him harshly. Love stayed, even as betrayal drew near. Then, taking the unleavened bread, Jesus gave thanks, broke it, and gave it to them, saying:

"Take, eat; this is My body."

—Matthew 26:26

This was more than bread. This was a declaration that the ancient Passover had been pointing to Him all along. He was the true Bread from heaven, broken for the salvation of many.

Then He took the cup and said:

"This is My blood of the new covenant, which is shed for many for the remission of sins."

—Matthew 26:28

Here, Jesus was fulfilling Jeremiah 31:31–34—the promise of a new covenant, written not on tablets of stone, but on hearts. But the spiritual conflict had not ended—it was only intensifying. Luke tells us that even at the table, the disciples argued over who was the greatest (Luke 22:24). Jesus responded not with rebuke, but by kneeling in humility to wash their feet (John 13:4–17). The Master served the servants. The King stooped low. He was preparing them not just to remember Him—but to become like Him.

Even Peter, full of confidence, was warned:

"Simon, Simon! Indeed, Satan has asked for you, that he may sift you as wheat. But I have prayed for you..."

—Luke 22:31–32

There it is again—spiritual warfare. Just as Satan entered Judas, now he wanted to sift Peter. But here is the difference: Jesus prayed for Peter. And though Peter would fall, he would be restored.

Conclusion: A Call to the Reader's Heart.

As we linger in the Upper Room, we are brought face to face with betrayal, love, pride, humility, failure, and grace. Every soul at that table is us. The traitor. The proud. The fearful. The broken. And yet Jesus, knowing all, chose to love, serve, and die for them.

Will you betray Him for the world's gain?

Will you deny Him when pressured?

Or will you surrender, broken, and receive the cup of His covenant?

The cross is drawing near. The Lamb has spoken. The door to mercy is open.

Prayer:

My Father;

I see myself at that table—uncertain, frail, proud, and yet invited. You served Your betrayer. You washed the feet of the denier. You loved to the end. Break my pride, pierce my heart, and lead me to repentance. I no longer want to follow You in name only, but in spirit and truth.

I receive Your broken body. I receive the blood of Your covenant. Write Your law upon my heart. I surrender oh Lord in the Holy name of Jesus, Amen.

CHAPTER 11: THE KISS OF BETRAYAL

The upper room was dimly lit. The smell of unleavened bread and bitter herbs still lingered as the disciples sat stunned. Jesus had just instituted something new—something sacred: the New Covenant in His blood. But as the atmosphere thickened with awe, Jesus 'next words pierced the silence like a dagger:

"Assuredly, I say to you that one of you who eats with Me will betray Me."

—Mark 14:18

Each disciple looked around nervously. The room that had moments before filled with worship now filled with suspicion, sorrow, and fear. And then Jesus turned to Peter—the boldest, the loudest, the most self-assured among them—and made a shocking prophecy:

"Simon, Simon! Indeed, Satan has asked for you, that he may sift you as wheat.

But I have prayed for you, that your faith should not fail.

and when you have returned to Me, strengthen your brethren."

—Luke 22:31–32

Peter, ever confident in his loyalty, responded with full assurance:

"Lord, I am ready to go with You, both to prison and to death."

—Luke 22:33

Jesus 'reply must have stunned him:

"I tell you, Peter, the rooster shall not crow this day before you will deny three times that you know Me."

—Luke 22:34

And in Matthew's account, Peter boldly insisted:

"Even if I have to die with You, I will not deny You!"

—Matthew 26:35

The contrast between Peter's self-confidence and Jesus 'prophetic foreknowledge could not be clearer. Peter loved Jesus as a friend and not as Lord Jesus on to death. He honestly believed he

would stand strong. But Jesus knew something Peter did not —how weak the flesh becomes when the cross draws near.

The Greek Layers: Satan's Request and Sifting,

In Luke 22:31, the Greek word translated "asked" (exēitēsato, ἐξῃτήσατο) implies a demand or legal petition. Satan was not simply requesting Peter for temptation—he was demanding to test him like Job. To sift (siniazō, σινιάζω) means to shake violently, to agitate like wheat in a sieve, separating what is useful from what is not. Peter was about to be tested in a spiritual trial. And though his love was real, his courage would collapse under the pressure. But Jesus did not leave him in despair—He told him, "I have prayed for you." Even before Peter fell, Jesus interceded for him. What a powerful truth: Jesus sees our failure before it happens and already stands as our Advocate before the Father.

A Prayer in the Garden

O Father in Heaven,

Here I am, trembling beside the shadowed trees of Gethsemane.

I have watched the Savior fall to the ground, face buried in the dust He once breathed into man. I have heard His sobs pierce the silence of night.

I have seen the blood in His sweat, the agony in His soul.

How could Love cry like that… for me?

Lord Jesus,

You knew the bitter taste of the cup—

You saw the wrath, the shame, the curse, the cross.

You investigated the abyss and still whispered, "Not My will, but Yours be done."

You chose obedience when disobedience was easier.

You chose the nails when You could have summoned angels. You chose me… when I was still choosing sin.

Break my heart, O God, as Yours broke.

Let not this moment pass without my full surrender.

No more halfway devotion, no more sleeping while You suffer.

Wake me up from spiritual slumber.

Teach me to watch. Teach me to pray.

Let me not deny You with my silence, nor betray You with a kiss of religion. Today, I lay down my will.

Today, I lay down my sin.

Today, I give You my heart—not in part, but whole.

If I have never known You, I kneel now at the cross, weeping and believing: You are the Son of God, my Savior, my Lord.

Take my life. Crush what must be crushed. Uproot what must be uprooted.

Raise what must be raised.

Cleanse my heart with your precious blood.

Now file my heart with the Awe and Fear of your Holiness.

And walk with me—through every Gethsemane—until the day I see Your face, oh Holy one I

pray in the name of Jesus, the Lamb of God, Amen.

Betrayed with a Kiss:

The moment had come. The sound of torches crackling and footsteps in the distance broke the stillness of Gethsemane. The Lord Jesus, rising from the agony of prayer, stood face to face with betrayal. He who had just said, "The hour has come," now saw it unfold before His eyes.

"And while He was still speaking, behold, Judas, one of the twelve, with a great multitude with swords and clubs, came from the chief priests and elders of the people."

— Matthew 26:47

One of the twelve. Not a stranger. Not a soldier. One of His own.

Judas had walked with Jesus. Heard His teachings. Saw His miracles. Dipped bread in the same bowl. Yet now, for thirty pieces of silver—the price of a slave—he handed over the Son of God. And how did he do it?

With a kiss.

"But Jesus said to him, 'Judas, are you betraying the Son of Man with a kiss?'"

—Luke 22:48

A kiss, the symbol of affection, twisted into the signal of treason. The sting of betrayal came not from a Roman spear, but from the lips of a disciple. The holy was handed over by one who had once called Him "Master."

Yet Jesus was not caught off guard. He did not flinch or flee. He stepped forward and said:

"I am He."

—John 18:5

At His words, the soldiers drew back and fell to the ground (John 18:6). Even in chains, He

revealed His authority.

He allowed Himself to be arrested. Why? Because the Scriptures had to be fulfilled. Because the Lamb had to be led to the slaughter. Because our redemption required it.

"But all this was done that the Scriptures of the prophets might be fulfilled."

—Matthew 26:56

The Silent Lamb Before the Shearers.

After the betrayal came the binding. The eternal Word, through whom all things were made, allowed sinful hands to seize Him. He was led like a lamb to the slaughter—yet not once did He resist. He did not raise His voice in protest. The only thing louder than the false accusations hurled at Him was His silence.

"He was oppressed, and He was afflicted, Yet He opened not His mouth.

He was led as a lamb to the slaughter, And as a sheep before its shearers is silent, So, He opened not His mouth."

— Isaiah 53:7

The religious leaders sought false testimony to put Him to death, but none could agree (Matthew 26:59–60). Lies piled upon lies, but Jesus remained silent, fulfilling the prophecy. He was questioned, mocked, and struck—yet He bore it all with divine restraint.

Finally, the high priest asked, "Are You the Christ, the Son of the Blessed?"

And Jesus, who had still been silent, now speaks—not to defend Himself, but to declare the truth.

"I am. And you will see the Son of Man sitting at the right hand of the Power and coming with the clouds of heaven."

— Mark 14:62

That declaration sealed their intent to kill Him. Yet what they did not know is that it also confirmed the plan of God.The Lamb of God was on His way to the cross—not as a victim of circumstance, but as the fulfillment of destiny.

Reflective Prayer: A Heart Awakened.

O Lamb of God, silent before Your accusers,

Pierced by betrayal, yet unwavering in Your purpose— How can I remain unmoved?

You were struck so I could be healed.

You were bound so I could be free.

You were rejected so I could be accepted.

Forgive me, Lord—for the many times I have kissed You with my lips but betrayed You with my life. Break the hardness of my heart. Let the weight of Your suffering awaken in me a fresh reverence, a holy fear, and a longing to follow You fully.

If I have never truly known You—Jesus, Son of God, have mercy on me. I believe you died for my sins and rose again.

I surrender. Be my Savior. Be my Lord in the name of Jesus, Amen.

CHAPTER 12: BEFORE THE ROOSTER CROWS

One of the greatest misunderstandings in Christian tradition is the belief that Jesus Christ was crucified on a Friday. But as we return to the Scriptures and examine the Jewish reckoning of days—beginning at sunset—we discover a much deeper truth, one that aligns perfectly with prophecy and divine timing.

According to the Jewish calendar, the day begins at sunset, not midnight. This means that what we often refer to as "Wednesday" in the Gregorian calendar began Tuesday evening for the Jews. It is on this day—after sunset—that Judas Iscariot went to the chief priests to betray the Lord, setting in motion the chain of events that would lead to the crucifixion.

This day was the preparation day before the Passover. But not just any Sabbath—it was a High Sabbath, a holy feast day according to the Law of Moses (see John 19:31). It was not the weekly Sabbath that falls on our Saturday. This distinction is vital.

"Therefore, because it was the Preparation Day, that the bodies should not remain on the cross on the Sabbath (for that Sabbath was a high day), the Jews asked Pilate that their legs might be broken, and that they might be taken away."

—John 19:31 NKJV

The gospel writers were precise. Both Matthew 26:17 and Mark 14:12 tell us that this was "the first day of Unleavened Bread, when they killed the Passover lamb." The timing is not symbolic—it is prophetic. Jesus, the true Passover Lamb (1 Corinthians 5:7), had to be sacrificed at the exact time the lambs were slain for the feast. The tradition of a Friday crucifixion contradicts the only sign Jesus gave to confirm His messiahship:

"For as Jonah was three days and three nights in the belly of the great fish, so will the Son of Man be three days and three nights in the heart of the earth" (Matthew 12:40).

A Friday death and Sunday morning resurrection simply does not add up to three full days and nights. But a crucifixion on Wednesday—beginning just after Tuesday's sunset—perfectly fulfills this prophecy.

This is not just a matter of calendar—it is a matter of divine accuracy. God's timeline is precise. Jesus fulfilled every feast and every prophecy exactly. The modern church must return to the Word and remove the veil of tradition that has covered the beauty of God's perfect timing.

The Night of Injustice: Jesus Before the High Priest

After Judas betrayed Him with a kiss, Jesus was seized in the Garden of Gethsemane and led under cover of night to the house of Annas, the former high priest, and then to Caiaphas, the current high priest (John 18:13, Matthew 26:57). What unfolded was not just an illegal trial—it was a spiritual and prophetic confrontation between darkness and Light.

This took place during the night hours of Tuesday, after sunset—meaning, according to the Jewish reckoning of time, it was already

Wednesday, the 14th of Nisan, the day of preparation for the Passover.

There, in the house of the high priest, the sinless Son of God was subjected to:

- False witnesses brought in to condemn Him, violating the Torah which requires truthful, agreeing testimony (Deuteronomy 19:15). Yet their words did not agree (Mark 14:56– 59).
- An illegal nighttime trial, which Jewish law forbade for capital offenses. Trials were to be conducted in the daylight, publicly, and with fairness.
- Physical abuse—He was spat upon, blindfolded, beaten, and mocked by those who held Him (Luke 22:63–65). They taunted Him, saying, "Prophesy! Who is the one who struck You?"

In this moment, the humility and silence of Jesus speak louder than any defense could. As Isaiah prophesied:

"I gave My back to those who struck Me, and My cheeks to those who plucked out the beard; I did not hide My face from shame and spitting."

—Isaiah 50:6

And again:

"He was oppressed, and He was afflicted, yet He opened not His mouth."

—Isaiah 53:7

When Caiaphas demanded, "Tell us if You are the Christ, the Son of God," Jesus answered:

"It is as you said. Nevertheless, I say to you, hereafter you will see the Son of Man sitting at the right hand of the Power and coming on the clouds of heaven."

— Matthew 26:64

This declaration sealed their hatred. Caiaphas tore his robes and accused Jesus of blasphemy— yet they were rejecting the very One their Scriptures foretold.

The Silence of Heaven and the Roar of Sin

As Jesus was mocked, spat upon, and held in custody, Peter—the bold disciple who had vowed to die with Him—was outside denying Him three times before the rooster crowed, just as Jesus had predicted.

The weight of this moment cannot be overstated.

- The priests who should have recognized the Messiah were conspiring to kill Him.
- The disciple who said he would never leave Him was weeping in bitter regret.
- The people were asleep while the Son of God endured the darkest night in history.

And yet, everything was unfolding exactly as it was foretold.

"The Son of Man indeed goes just as it is written of Him, but woe to that man by whom the Son of Man is betrayed! It would have been good for that man if he had never been born." "

— Mark 14:21 NKJV

Heaven was not silent because it was indifferent. Heaven was silent because the Lamb had to be offered. He had to endure the cup of wrath alone.

Peter's Denial: When Fear Drowns Faith

While Jesus was enduring false accusations, beatings, and humiliations inside the high priest's house, Peter stood outside, trying to stay close—

yet at a distance. His heart must have been torn between loyalty and fear, between love and self-preservation.

Only hours before, he had boldly declared:

"Even if I have to die with You, I will not deny You!"

— Matthew 26:35

But Jesus, with eyes that saw the heart, had already warned him:

"Assuredly, I say to you that this night, before the rooster crows, you will deny Me three times."

— Matthew 26:34

And now, just as Jesus was being ridiculed by His enemies, Peter was being identified by his bystanders. First, a servant girl said, "You also were with Jesus of Galilee." But he denied it— "I do not know what you are saying." Then another said, "This fellow also was with Jesus of Nazareth." Again, he denied it with an oath— "I do not know the Man!" Finally, others around him said, "Surely you also are one of them, for your speech betrays you." Then Peter began to curse and to swear, saying, "I do not know the Man!"

"Then he began to curse and swear, saying, "I do not know the Man!" Immediately a rooster crowed. And Peter remembered the word of Jesus who had said to him, "Before the rooster crows, you will deny Me three times." So, he went out and wept bitterly."

— Matthew 26:74-75 NKJV

The Rooster's Cry and the Savior's Eyes,

Luke gives us a powerful detail:

"Then the Lord turned and looked at Peter. Then Peter

remembered the word of the Lord..."

— Luke 22:61

Can you imagine that moment? Jesus bruised and bound—yet still full of love—turns to look at Peter. Not with condemnation, but with a look that says, "I told you this would happen. But I still love you. I still chose you." Peter's heart broke. He ran out into the night and wept bitterly—not because he got caught, but because he betrayed the One who loved him most.

Why This Moment Matters!

Peter's failure was not final. Jesus had prayed for him in advance:

"But I have prayed for you, that your faith should not fail; and when you have returned to Me, strengthen your brethren."

— Luke 22:32

Jesus knew Peter's weakness, and He made provision for his restoration. The same is true for us. Many today deny Jesus—not always with words, but by their silence, by their compromise, by choosing comfort over truth. This part of Peter's story is a mirror. It shows us that no one is strong enough on their own. Even the most zealous heart can stumble. But repentance is not the end—it is the beginning of restoration.

Reflection and Call

Have you denied Him in your own way?

Maybe you once walked closely with Jesus, but fear, shame, or the pressure of others made you drift. You have stayed in the courtyard, trying to follow Him from a distance—watching, but not surrendering.

Jesus is looking at you now—not with condemnation, but with love. The same love that restored Peter. The same love that took Him to the cross.

Will you weep in repentance as Peter did?

Will you return and follow Him with all your heart?

The rooster has crowed. But grace is still calling.

A Prayer of Returning:

Father,

I see myself in Peter.

I have claimed loyalty with my lips, but in moments of fear and weakness,

I have denied You by my silence, my compromise, my distance. You saw it all.

And yet, like Peter, you look at me—not with wrath, but with mercy. Your eyes pierce my heart and call me back.

Forgive me, Lord.

Cleanse me from every sin of denial, every fear-driven failure. Let my bitter weeping turn to true repentance,

and my brokenness become the foundation of deeper devotion.

You prayed for Peter—and You intercede for me now. Strengthen me to return.

To follow You not from a distance, but up close—no matter the cost. I surrender again.

Not just my words, but my whole heart.

In Your Holy name, Jesus, Amen.

CHAPTER 13: WHAT IS TRUTH? THE KING BEFORE PILATE

By this time in the divine timeline, we are now on the day before the Passover, which fell on the 14th of Nisan—our Tuesday evening to Wednesday sunset by Jewish reckoning. Remember, a Jewish day begins at sundown, not midnight, as per Genesis 1:5: "So the evening and the morning were the first day."

This distinction is critical.

What the Church in Rome later labeled as "Good Friday" was in fact not the day of the crucifixion. Jesus was not crucified on a Friday before a regular weekly Sabbath (Saturday), but on a Wednesday, before a High Sabbath, which was the Feast of Unleavened Bread—a special annual Sabbath that began the evening of Passover (John 19:31). The saying Good Friday was a saying established by the Jaws who wanted the Lord Jesus crucified, and after His death on Wednesday at exactly 3 pm it became a celebration chant, they called it a good day because Jesus who they considered a blasphemer and an evil man was now no more.

But through religious deception and polarization of the word of God by the Roman Catholic Church who established a Friday crucifixion of the Lord Jesus Christ, because the Roma Catholic Church was the only authority over Christians all over the world for centuries, they had the power and authority to manipulate the true authority of the word of God to establish there own doctrines and the systems of worship to suit the worship of there gods. True worship of the one and only true God was combined with the worship of Roman gods to become one world religion.

The mystery of deception and lawlessness is already at work, one world religion, one world political system, one world government and one world leader. This is unfolding right in our eyes.

The Lord Jesus Christ is sounding an alarm trough His word!

"And I heard another voice from heaven saying, "Come out of her, my people, lest you share in her sins, and lest you receive of her plagues."

— Revelation 18:4 NKJV

"Depart! Depart! Go out from there, touch no unclean thing; Go out from the midst of her, be clean, you who bear the vessels of the Lord."

— Isaiah 52:11 NKJV

""My people, go out of the midst of her! And let everyone deliver himself from the fierce anger of the Lord."

— Jeremiah 51:45 NKJV

I have much to say about the Catholic Church, but it is not the purpose for this book.

The confusion stems from a failure to distinguish between a weekly Sabbath and a High Sabbath, and centuries of church tradition have replaced Scripture with assumption. But Jesus 'own words settle the timeline:

"For as Jonah was three days and three nights in the belly of the great fish, so will the Son of Man be three days and three nights in the heart of the earth."

— Matthew 12:40 NKJV

From Wednesday afternoon to Saturday evening, you get three days and three nights—just as He said. It was after midnight, early on Wednesday morning, that Jesus was arrested and taken from Gethsemane to the house of the high priest. He had already been betrayed by Judas, arrested by the temple guards, and abandoned by most of His disciples. Peter had denied Him. The hour of darkness was fully underway.

Now, bruised and bound, Jesus is brought before the most powerful man in Judea—Pontius Pilate, the Roman governor. But though Pilate had authority in the earthly sense, he stood before the very Word of God made flesh—the One through whom all authority exists.

"You could have no power at all against Me unless it had been given you from above."

—John 19:11

Here, in this courtroom of politics, fear, and manipulation, Truth stood on trial.

And yet, it was not Jesus being judged—it was the world. Pilate asked the question of the ages:

"What is truth?" (John 18:38)

But Truth was standing right in front of him.

The Trial Before Pilate: A Collision of Kingdoms

After a sleepless night of unjust trials before Annas and Caiaphas,

Jesus—already beaten and mocked—was taken early in the morning to Pilate's judgment hall. The religious leaders refused to enter the governor's headquarters, lest they be defiled and unable to eat the Passover (John 18:28), revealing their hypocrisy: they were obsessed with ceremonial cleanliness while plotting the murder of the sinless Lamb of God. Unfortunately, this is the state of many religious Christian's who outwardly show to be pure but inwardly they hearts are defiled with jealousy, envy, gossip, slander, and all sort of ungodliness. Remember the religious leaders wanted the Lord Jesus killed because of jealousy.

Pilate came out to them and asked, "What accusation do you bring against this Man?" (John 18:29)

Their response betrayed the truth:

"If He were not an evildoer, we would not have delivered Him up to you."

—John 18:30

Pilate could sense this was no ordinary criminal. In fact, after interrogating Jesus, he found no fault in Him (John 18:38). But the pressure from the crowd and the political climate forced him to waver.

"Are You the King of the Jews?" Pilate asked.

"My kingdom is not of this world," Jesus answered.

"You say rightly that I am a king. For this cause I was born, and for this cause I have come into the world, that I should bear witness to the truth.

Everyone who is of the truth hears My voice."

—John 18:36–37 NKJV

"Pilate said to Him, "What is truth?" And when he had said this, he went out again to the Jews, and said to them, "I find no fault in Him at all."

—John 18:38 NKJV

This moment was not only political—it was deeply prophetic. Isaiah had spoken of this:

"He was oppressed, and He was afflicted,

Yet He opened not His mouth.

He was led as a lamb to the slaughter."

—Isaiah 53:7

Jesus was calm, in control, and fully submitted to the Father's plan. While the leaders accused Him with rage, He offered no defense. His silence was not weakness—it was strength in surrender to the will of God.

The Choice: Barabbas or Jesus?

Pilate, seeing a way to escape responsibility, offered the crowd a Passover tradition: to release one prisoner. He presented a notorious rebel and murderer named Barabbas, and the innocent Christ.

"Whom do you want me to release to you? Barabbas, or Jesus who is called Christ?"

—Matthew 27:17

The name Barabbas means "son of the father" (Bar = son, Abba = father), a dark irony: the people chose a false son of the father over the true Son of the Father.

The crowd shouted:

"Not this Man, but Barabbas!" (John 18:40)

In that moment, the guilt of all humanity echoed through the square. It was not just the crowd—it was us all who rejected the Righteous One.

Behold the Man!

Pilate had Jesus scourged, hoping the brutal beating would appease the crowd. The soldiers twisted together a crown of thorns and mocked Him, draping Him in a purple robe.

"Hail, King of the Jews!" they cried, as they struck Him.

Then Pilate brought Him out and said those haunting words:

"Behold the Man!"

—John 19:5

What a sight it must have been—bloodied, bruised, silent. The Lamb of God standing ready for sacrifice. Not just for Israel. But for you.

Pilate tried again to release Him, but the chief priests cried out:

"If you let this Man, go, you are not Caesar's friend!" (John 19:12)

And when Pilate sat in the judgment seat, they said:

"We have no king but Caesar!" (John 19:15)

In that chilling moment, the religious leaders sealed their rejection of the Messiah and their covenant with Rome. The True King had come—and they cast Him out.

A Closing Reflection:

Jesus stood silent before His accusers, so that we could be declared righteous before the Judge of all.

He wore a crown of thorns, so that we could receive a crown of life.

Men rejected him, so that we might be accepted by the Father.

The Scourging: A Soldier's Sport

1. Binding to the Pillar

Jesus was stripped to His undergarments and tied to a stone pillar in the praetorium courtyard. His arms raised, chest exposed—every breath a struggle against the straps that cut into His wrists.

2. The Flagrum (Flagellum)

In each hand, a soldier held a short leather whip, its end laden with metal balls and shark-like bone or lead weights. Known as the flagrum, it turned each lash into a tearing, lacerating stroke.

3. Thirty-Nine Strips

Jewish law limited scourging to forty lashes (Deuteronomy 25:3), so Roman practice

borrowed the number thirty-nine to avoid transgressing that limit. Yet it was seldom meted out humanely. Each blow drove metal and bone into flesh, ripping muscle and sinew.

4. The Dance of Cruelty

The soldiers worked with brutal choreography—one holding skin taut on Jesus's back, the other raining down lashes in rapid succession. Encouraged by jeers, they even paused now and then to twist the whip, ensuring deeper tear and bleed.

5. Blood and Sorrow

Blood ran in rivulets down His back and pooled at His feet. Pain so exquisite that every breath felt like a burning brand. Sweat, dirt, and blood blurred His vision—but still He did not cry out.

The Prophecy Fulfilled

Isaiah spoke of this very suffering centuries before:

"But He was wounded for our transgressions.

He was bruised for our iniquities.

The chastisement for our peace was upon Him, And by His stripes we are healed."

—Isaiah 53:5

Here, "stripes" (the Hebrew maḵot) refer to the very wounds inflicted by that whip. The Lamb of God—without sin—endured the lash so that we might know peace with the Father. Every crimson thread of His flesh was a thread in the tapestry of our redemption.

The Silent Savior:

Throughout the scourging, Jesus did not defend Himself. He did not curse His tormentors. His silence echoed Isaiah's words:

"He was oppressed, and He was afflicted, yet He opened not His mouth."

—Isaiah 53:7

He stood alone—God incarnate—bearing in His body the full weight of our sin, our guilt, our curse.

A Prayer of Reverent Awe!

O Holy Lamb,

I tremble to imagine the agony of Your flesh.

Each lash You endured was for my healing—my peace with the Father. Forgive me for the times I have taken Your sacrifice for granted.

Break my heart for what broke Yours.

May the memory of Your stripes keep me ever grateful, ever humble,

And ever longing to proclaim your grace in your precious name, Jesus, Amen.

CHAPTER 14: THE FINAL STROLL - (GOLGOTHA)

After the Roman soldiers finished scourging Jesus, His body broken and torn. Yet their cruelty did not end there. According to Matthew 27, Mark 15, Luke 23, and John 19, they continued to mock Him:

"Then the soldiers of the governor took Jesus into the Praetorium and gathered the whole garrison around Him.

And they stripped Him and put a scarlet robe on Him. When they had twisted a crown of thorns, they put it on His head, and a reed in His right hand. And they bowed the knee before Him and mocked Him, saying, 'Hail, King of the Jews! 'Then they spat on Him, took the reed, and struck Him on the head."

—Matthew 27:27–30 NKJV

The crown of thorns was not merely a mockery—it was agony. The thorns were long and sharp, from the jujube tree, and they were pressed into His scalp. Blood would have flowed down His face, mixing with sweat, spittle, and the dust of death.

The scarlet robe, thrown over His raw back, clung to His wounds and later tore them open again when removed. Every act of mockery fulfilled the words of prophecy:

"I gave My back to those who struck Me,

And My cheeks to those who plucked out the beard.

I did not hide My face from shame and spitting."

—Isaiah 50:6

The Via Dolorosa – The Way of Suffering:

After this humiliation, Jesus was handed over to be crucified. Roman law required the condemned to carry their own crossbeam (patibulum) to the execution site. This beam, weighing up to 100 pounds, was laid across Jesus 'shoulders—already torn and bleeding.

"And He, bearing His cross, went out to a place called the Place of a Skull, which is called in Hebrew, Golgotha."

—John 19:17 NKJV

But His strength gave way. The scourging had drained Him. Collapsing under the weight, Jesus could no longer carry the beam alone.

"Now as they came out, they found a man of Cyrene, Simon by name. Him they compelled to bear His cross."

—Matthew 27:32

Simon of Cyrene, just arriving in Jerusalem for the feast, suddenly found himself carrying the burden of the world's sin—not in truth, but in shadow. And yet, how fitting that the man who carried the cross was from Cyrene—North Africa—foreshadowing the Gospel reaching the Gentile world.

The Women Who Wept!

On the road to Golgotha, a group of women—faithful followers—watched with broken hearts.

"But Jesus, turning to them, said, 'Daughters of Jerusalem, do not weep for Me, but weep for yourselves and for your children.'"

—Luke 23:28

Even in His agony, Jesus was thinking of others—warning them of the judgment to come. This prophecy pointed to the destruction of Jerusalem in 70AD, but it also echoes the greater sorrow of rejecting the Messiah.

Reflection and Prayer:

O Jesus,

The weight You bore was not just a beam of wood, But the sins of every man and woman, including mine. How can I ever understand such love?

You, the King of glory, allowed Yourself to be mocked and mutilated. Let me never treat lightly what cost You everything.

Let me weep not only for Your pain, but for the sins that nailed You there.

Teach me to take up my cross daily and follow You,

Not in pride, but in humility I pray in your Holy name Jesus.

Numbered Among Transgressors:

As Jesus, bruised and bloodied from Roman scourging, out of the Praetorium bearing His cross, He was not led alone:

"There were also two others, evildoers, led with Him to be put to death."

—Luke 23:32 NKJV

These "evildoers" (kakourgoi in the Greek) were condemned criminals, already sentenced and prepared for execution alongside Jesus. They were led with Him—not after Him, not separately, but with Him, which means they shared in the public procession from the judgment hall toward Golgotha. Jesus was counted among them from the very beginning of the death march, fulfilling Isaiah's prophecy:

"Therefore I will divide Him a portion with the great, And He shall divide the spoil with the strong, Because He poured out His soul unto death, And He was numbered with the transgressors, And He bore the sin of many, And made intercession for the transgressors."

— Isaiah 53:12 NKJV

Luke describes them as kakourgoi, a term denoting criminal guilt—broad enough to include a variety of offenses. These two, as many scholars believe, are the same individuals who are later seen on crosses beside Jesus, one of whom would repent and call upon the Lord even in his final hour.

But Matthew adds a detail that shifts the scene slightly further:

"Then they crucified Him, and divided His garments, casting lots...

Then two robbers were crucified with Him, one on the right and another on the left."

—Matthew 27:35, 38 NKJV

Here we see a slightly different sequence. First, Jesus is crucified, then His garments are parted and lots cast, and after that, two robbers (lēstai) are crucified beside Him.

This opens a fascinating possibility—one that aligns with my insight: the two "evildoers" in Luke 23:32 were led with Jesus, while the "robbers" in Matthew 27:38 were brought later.

Two sets of criminals?

Could it be that Jesus was not crucified between two criminals (as traditionally understood), but that two other robbers were added to the crucifixion site after Jesus was already nailed to the cross? So this is my thought the two criminal's who were led with the Lord Jesus were crucified at the same time one on the right and one on the left then the other two robbers were brought after the parting of His garment and crucified one further outward of the one criminal on the right side and the other robber on the other criminal further outward on the left side. Something to ponder about and to consider. This is why I love the word of God; I love searching the Holy scriptures. To further support my insight let us look at what the gospel of John says to hit the nail on the head.

"Therefore, because it was the Preparation Day, that the bodies should not remain on the cross on the Sabbath (for that Sabbath was a high day), the Jews asked Pilate that their legs might be broken, and that they might be taken away. Then the soldiers came and broke the legs of the first and of the other who was crucified with Him. But when they came to Jesus and saw that He was already dead, they did not break His legs. But one of the soldiers pierced His side with a spear, and immediately blood and water came out."

—John 19:31-34 NKJV

It clearly says that the soldiers came and broke the legs of the first(The robber who was brought after the parting of the garment and was crucified next outward to the criminal who was led with and crucified next to the Lord Jesus) so the soldiers broke the first robber's legs and then came and broke the criminal's legs then by the time they got to the Lord Jesus

Christ they saw that He was already dead, they did not break His legs but to prove that He was dead the soldiers pierced His side with a spear, and immediately blood and water came out fulfilling prophecy.

"For these things were done that the Scripture should be fulfilled, "Not one of His bones shall be broken." And again, another Scripture says, "They shall look on Him whom they pierced.""

— John 19:36-37 NKJV

"He guards all his bones; Not one of them is broken." Psalms 34:20 NKJV

The Greek word used in Matthew 27:38—λῃσταί (lēstai)—carries the idea of violent criminals, revolutionaries, or insurrectionists. This is the same word used for Barabbas in John 18:40, a more politically charged, Zealot-like background. This could mean these "robbers" were of a different criminal class than the "evildoers" in the gospel of Luke.

And most significantly: Matthew places their crucifixion after the casting of lots for Jesus' garments—after Jesus already nailed on the cross.

This makes a profound point:

Jesus was not simply crucified with common criminals. As the scene progressed, other robbers were added, surrounding Him with increasing shame, injustice, and prophetic fulfillment.

Fulfilled Prophecy, Layer by Layer

- Led with criminals (Luke 23:32) – Isaiah 53:12 fulfilled.
- Crucified, then His garments parted (Matthew 27:35) – Psalm 22:18 fulfilled.
- Surrounded by robbers on either side (Matthew 27:38) – Amplifying His humiliation, also reflecting Psalm 22:16:

"For dogs have surrounded Me; the congregation of the wicked has enclosed Me. They pierced My hands and My feet."

And the Word "Others" in Luke 23:32?

"Two others also, evildoers, were led with Him to be put to death."

The word for "others" is ἕτεροι (heteroi), which means others of a different kind. This may subtly emphasize that Jesus was distinct from those He was crucified alongside—a sinless man among the guilty. The Greek nuance reinforces the theological reality: though treated as one of them, He was not one of them. He bore their sins but committed none.

As Jesus hung nailed to the cross, arms stretched wide and flesh torn open, He did not curse those who hurt Him. He did not plead for deliverance. He did not call down judgment.

He prayed:

"Then Jesus said, "Father, forgive them, for they do not know what they do." And they divided His garments and cast lots."

— Luke 23:34 NKJV

This prayer pierces the veil between heaven and earth. It is not just a historical moment—it is a personal invitation. At His most vulnerable, Jesus displayed the heart of God: a heart that forgives, intercedes, and loves beyond comprehension.

He prayed this not only for the Roman soldiers, but for the priests who handed Him over, for the crowd who shouted, "Crucify Him!" and yes—for you and me.

It is easy to distance ourselves from the scene and imagine we would have done differently. But the truth is, our sin nailed Him there just as surely as the soldier's hammer. Yet He did not resist. He willingly bore it, and He forgave.

This is grace. This is mercy. This is love nailed to a cross.

A Prayer for the Reader:

Lord Jesus,

I can hardly understand the depth of Your love. As You hung in agony, you thought not of Yourself but of those who caused Your pain. You asked the Father to forgive. And You still do—for me.

I confess my sins. I see my guilt. And i fall before Your mercy.

Break my heart for what breaks Yours. Let Your prayer become my salvation. I receive Your forgiveness. I surrender to Your love.

Be my Savior. Be my Lord in the name of Jesus I pray. Amen.

Reflection: Which Side of the Cross Are You On?

The cross of Christ stood between two condemned men—one cursed the Savior, the other cried out for mercy. In this divine moment, we see that proximity to Jesus is not enough. Both criminals were equally close to Him in death, but only one saved. What made the difference?

Humility. Repentance. Faith.

This scene forces us to ask: Which side of the cross am I on? Have I hardened my heart in pride and self-justification?

Or will I, like the repentant thief, confess my sin and reach out to the only One who can save?

The grace Jesus offered to the dying criminal is the same grace extended to you—today. Not tomorrow. Not once you have fixed yourself. But now, in your brokenness. In your need.

The cross is still the great divide—between the proud and the humble, between judgment and mercy, between eternal separation and eternal life.

Prayer: A Cry from the Cross

Lord Jesus,

I see You there bloodied, bruised, and yet full of compassion.

I hear Your voice whispering mercy even to the most undeserving. I confess, I am that criminal. Guilty. Broken. In need of grace.

Remember me, Lord, not for my works, but for Your mercy. Cleanse me with the blood You shed.

Make me new by the power of Your resurrection.

Today, I turn my heart to You. Be my Savior. Be my King.

I choose life at the foot of Your cross. Amen.

CHAPTER 15: THE CRUCIFIED KING

As the sun rose on the 14th of Nisan—Wednesday by Jewish reckoning—the Lamb of God, without blemish and without spot, lifted between heaven and earth. The Son of Man, beaten and bloodied, now nailed to a Roman pole at Golgotha. This was not just another execution—this was the fulfillment of prophecy. From the foundations of the world, He was the Lamb slain (Revelation 13:8).

"And when they had come to the place called Calvary, there they crucified Him, and the

criminals, one on the right hand and the other on the left."

— Luke 23:33 NKJV

He was surrounded by transgressors, just as Isaiah had foretold: "And He was numbered with the transgressors" (Isaiah 53:12). But even in His agony, He opened not His mouth in complaint, only in compassion. His first words on the cross were not of judgment, but of mercy: "Father, forgive them, for they do not know what they do" (Luke 23:34). Who can understand such love?

The darkness that soon covered the land from the sixth hour (12pm) to the ninth hour (3pm) (Matthew 27:45) was not only a physical sign, but a spiritual reality. The Light of the world was rejected, and creation itself mourned.

Let us now walk through these final hours of the Lord—not merely as readers of history, but as participants in the grief, glory, and grace of redemption.

The Final Hours of the Cross:

The Gospel accounts tell us that Jesus was crucified at the third hour (Mark 15:25), which is approximately 9:00 a.m. in Jewish time reckoning. Then, something profound happens:

"Now from the sixth hour until the ninth hour there was darkness over all the land."

—Matthew 27:45 (NKJV)

In Jewish timekeeping, the sixth hour is 12:00 noon, and the ninth hour is 3:00 p.m. From noon until mid-afternoon, a supernatural darkness covered the land. This was not a solar eclipse—it was the middle of Passover, which always occurs during a full moon. This was divine mourning, a cosmic sign that something eternally significant was taking place.

Why This Darkness?

The darkness mirrors the ninth plague of Egypt (Exodus 10:21–23), when God covered the land with thick darkness just before the death of the firstborn. Here again, darkness precedes death— but this time, it is the death of God's only begotten Son, the true Firstborn from all creation (Colossians 1:15). The judgment that hovered over Egypt now hung-over Golgotha.

As Jesus bore the weight of our sin, the Father turned His face away. It was in this moment that Jesus cried out with brokenness deeper than physical pain:

"Eli, Eli, lama sabachthani?"

—that is, "My God, My God, why have You forsaken Me?"

—Matthew 27:46

This cry, quoting Psalm 22:1, was not a cry of confusion—it was a prophetic declaration. Psalm 22 not only begins with these words, but it details crucifixion centuries before it was ever practiced. From the mocking of bystanders, the piercing of hands and feet, the casting of lots for His garments—it was all there.

"My God, My God, why have You forsaken Me? Why are You so far from helping Me, And from the words of My groaning?"

— Psalms 22:1 NKJV

Jesus was not merely dying. He was fulfilling Scripture in perfect precision.

The Lamb's Final Words!

As the ninth hour approached, the work of redemption was coming to its climax. The Gospel of John records Jesus 'final victorious words:

"It is finished!"

—John 19:30

In the Greek, the word is "Tetelestai"—a legal and financial term meaning "Paid in full." This was not a cry of defeat, but of completion. The debt of sin settled. The wrath of God had been satisfied.

Luke records His last breath as a child entrusting Himself to His Father:

"Father, into Your hands I commit My spirit."

—Luke 23:46

And with that, He breathed His last.

The Earth Responds:

At that moment, the veil of the temple was torn from top to bottom (Matthew 27:51)—a divine act. The veil was not a thin curtain; it was a thick, embroidered barrier that separated the Holy of Holies, where God's presence dwelled. Only the high priest could enter it once a year on the Day of Atonement. But now, through the torn flesh of Christ, the way into God's presence opened— for all who believe.

"Therefore, brethren, having boldness to enter the Holiest by the blood of Jesus, by a new and living way which He consecrated for us, through the veil, that is, His flesh,"

— Hebrews 10:19-20 NKJV

There was also an earthquake, rocks split, and graves opened. The centurion and soldiers all trembled and declared:

"So when the centurion and those with him, who were guarding Jesus, saw the earthquake and the things that had happened, they feared greatly, saying, "Truly this was the Son of God!""

— Matthew 27:54 NKJV

Reflection: The Silent Grief of Those Who Loved Him

As Joseph and Nicodemus gently placed Jesus 'lifeless body in the tomb, the weight of sorrow pressed on all who loved Him. His mother, Mary, stood near — the same arms that once cradled Him in Bethlehem now empty, her heart pierced just as Simeon had prophesied decades earlier:

"(yes, a sword will pierce through your own soul also)' that the thoughts of many hearts may be revealed.""

— Luke 2:35 NKJV

She had followed Him through it all: the miracles, the teachings, the accusations — and now, she had watched Him suffer unspeakably and die. What does a mother do when her son, the Son of God, crucified?

She wept!

And what of the disciples? Scattered, confused, and shattered in spirit. The One who calmed storms, raised the dead, and spoke like no man ever had — was now silent in a tomb. Peter, who had sworn loyalty, had denied Him. John, the beloved disciple, stood at the foot of the cross but could do nothing to stop the horror. Thomas doubted. Judas was gone in darkness. The rest hid behind locked doors.

Their hopes had died on that cross. Their dreams buried in that tomb. Yet even in the depth of sorrow, God was not silent. Even in the stillness of death, His Word was working. Every tear would become testimony. Every heartache would turn to hope. Because Sunday was coming.

Closing Prayer:

Father, we thank You that You are near to the brokenhearted. As Mary wept and the disciples mourned, so too do we carry pain and questions in this life. But You see. You know. And You promise resurrection after sorrow. Thank You for the cross and thank You that the story does not end in the grave. We worship You — not only for what You have done but for who You are. In the name of Jesus, Amen.

CHAPTER 16: THE THIRD DAY- HE IS RISEN

From the moment Jesus laid in the tomb, time began ticking toward the most pivotal moment in human history—His resurrection. But to understand the depth and precision of this event, we must first rightly count the three days and three nights that Jesus Himself prophesied.

In Matthew 12:40, Jesus declares:

"For as Jonah was three days and three nights in the belly of the great fish, so will the Son of Man be three days and three nights in the heart of the earth."

This statement was prophetic and exact.

According to the Jewish reckoning of time, a day begins at sunset and ends at the following sunset (Genesis 1:5, Leviticus 23:32). Jesus buried just before sunset on what we now call Tuesday evening, which marked the start of Wednesday on the Jewish calendar. That day— Wednesday—was the preparation day before the High Sabbath of Passover, not the regular seventh-day Sabbath.

Here is how the timeline unfolds:

- Burial: Before sunset Tuesday (start of Wednesday)
- Night 1 & Day 1: Wednesday (High Sabbath) Passover
- Night 2 & Day 2: Thursday
- Night 3 & Day 3: Friday
- Resurrection: After sunset on Saturday, which began the first day of the week (Sunday)

Thus, Jesus rose after three literal days and nights, fulfilling His own words with divine precision. This corrects the common tradition that places His crucifixion on Friday and resurrection on Sunday morning—an interpretation that cannot account for three full days and nights.

Let us now step into the glory of His rising. The earth shook, the stone rolled away—not to let Him out, but to let us see in. Death had lost its sting. The grave conquered. Jesus had risen—just as He said.

He Is Risen!

As the Sabbath ended and the first day of the week began—after sunset on what we call Saturday evening—the tomb that had been sealed and guarded could no longer hold the Lord of life.

Matthew tells us:

"Now after the Sabbath, as the first day of the week began to dawn, Mary Magdalene and the other Mary came to see the tomb."

—Matthew 28:1 NKJV

The word translated "dawn" in this verse is epiphōskō in the Greek, which means "to begin to shine" or "to draw on." This was not sunrise but the beginning of the new day at sunset—in Jewish reckoning, the beginning of Sunday. The resurrection had already occurred by the time the women arrived at the tomb early Sunday morning. He had already risen—just after sunset Saturday!

The angel declared:

"He is not here; for He is risen, as He said."

—Matthew 28:6 NKJV

With this victorious announcement, the foundation of our faith sealed. Jesus Christ rose bodily from the grave. The Roman seal could not hold Him. The guards could not stop Him. Death could not defeat Him.

This moment changed everything.

Fulfillment of Prophecy:

Jesus had spoken repeatedly of His resurrection:

- "Destroy this temple, and in three days I will raise it up." (John 2:19)
- "The Son of Man must suffer many things…and be killed and be raised the third day." (Luke 9:22)

Even the religious leaders remembered His words and requested guards for the tomb, fearing the disciples might claim He had risen. But what they feared only confirmed the truth: He rose indeed!

Psalm 16:10 had prophesied:

"For You will not leave my soul in Sheol,

Nor will You allow Your Holy One to see corruption."

Jesus did not see decay. He rose before the third night had passed. His body never corrupted, for it was the Holy One.

The First Witness: Mary Magdalene

It was not to Peter, nor John, nor any of the Eleven that the risen Lord first appeared. It was to Mary Magdalene—a woman once bound by darkness, out of whom Jesus had cast seven demons (Luke 8:2). She had followed Him closely, served Him faithfully, and now she wept for Him deeply.

"But Mary stood outside by the tomb weeping, and as she wept,

she stooped down and looked into the tomb."

—John 20:11 NKJV

She was the last at the cross and the first at the tomb. Her love for the Lord had not faded with death—it only grew. The perfume she once poured on His feet now filled the air again with her broken sobs. She searched for Him, even though she thought Him dead.

And then, Jesus appeared.

"Jesus said to her, 'Mary!'

She turned and said to Him, 'Rabboni!' (which is to say, Teacher)."

—John 20:16 NKJV

No one had to tell her it was Him—she knew His voice.

This moment is not just intimate—it is prophetic. Her eyes, once filled with sorrow, now beheld the risen King. She became the first evangelist of the resurrection, sent by the Lord Himself to tell the disciples:

"Go to My brethren and say to them, 'I am ascending to My Father and your Father, and to My God and your God.'"

—John 20:17 NKJV

Why Mary?

The Lord's choice to appear first to Mary reveals so much:

- It affirms the depth of her love and loyalty—she lingered at the tomb when others had left.
- It shows the value Jesus placed on devotion over status—He chose a woman, not a prominent apostle, to proclaim His resurrection.
- It reflects the prophetic beauty of Isaiah 61:1–3, which Jesus fulfilled:

" "The Spirit of the Lord God is upon Me, Because the

Lord has anointed Me To preach good tidings to the poor; He has sent Me to heal the brokenhearted, To proclaim liberty to the captives, And the opening of the prison to those who are bound; To proclaim the acceptable year of the Lord, And the day of vengeance of our God; To comfort all who mourn, To console those who mourn in Zion, To give them beauty for ashes, The oil of joy for mourning, The garment of praise for the spirit of heaviness; That they may be called trees of righteousness, The planting of the Lord, that He may be glorified." "

—Isaiah 61:1-3 NKJV

Mary's weeping turned into worship. Her mourning swallowed up in joy.

let us not forget—the anointing she once poured on Jesus was not in vain. Jesus said:

"She has kept this for the day of My burial." (John 12:7)

She had understood what the others had missed. Her affection was more than emotion; it was rooted in revelation. Her devotion was born out of gratitude, deep love, and a brokenness made whole by His mercy.

The Torn Veil: God's Eternal Invitation

Now Jesus died on the cross, something happened in the temple that marked a shift in eternity:

"Then, behold, the veil of the temple was torn in two from top to bottom..."

—Matthew 27:51 NKJV

That veil, which separated the Holy of Holies from the rest of the temple, was a symbol of the separation between God and man due to sin. Only the high priest could enter once a year—and never without blood.

But now, the blood of Jesus had shed, and the veil was torn—not from bottom to top, as if by human effort, but from top to bottom, by the hand of God.

The resurrection sealed what the crucifixion had bought: access.

"Therefore, brethren, having boldness to enter the Holiest by the blood of Jesus, by a new and living way which He consecrated for us, through the veil, that is, His flesh..."

—Hebrews 10:19–20 NKJV

From the beginning—in Eden—God walked with man. That fellowship broken by sin, but the heart of God never changed. Through the tabernacle, the temple, and the prophets, He kept reaching. But it was only through Jesus, the perfect sacrifice, that the barrier was finally destroyed.

Jesus did not just rise from the grave—He opened the way back to the Father. And Mary Magdalene, once outcast and afflicted, was the first to see the new covenant in motion.

A Call to the Heart: Come Through the Veil

The veil has been torn.

The grave is empty.

He is risen.

From the garden of Eden to the garden tomb, God has been calling your name. The resurrection of Jesus Christ is not just a moment in history—it is a divine invitation. The barrier of sin that kept us far from God has removed. The blood had shed. The way is open.

Like Mary Magdalene, you may carry shame, grief, or wounds from your past. But Jesus calls you by name. He calls you to see the cross, the empty tomb, and the torn veil—and to step into restored fellowship with God.

"For through Him we both have access by one Spirit to the Father."

—Ephesians 2:18 NKJV

This is not religion. This is not ritual. This is redemption. This is a return to the One who formed you, knows you, and longs for you. If you have never surrendered your life to Jesus Christ, this is your moment. He died for you, He rose for you, and He is calling you to come.

Pray from your heart:

"Lord Jesus, I believe you died for my sins and rose again. I turn away from everything that has separated me from You. Tear down every veil in my heart. Forgive me, cleanse me, and receive me. I want to walk with You. I want to know You. From this moment, I give You, my life. Be my Savior and my Lord. Amen."

If you are already a believer but have drifted, let this chapter remind you: the veil is still torn. Return. Draw near. Worship. Fellowship with the Father has been restored through the son.

He is calling.

Will you come?

CHAPTER 17: THE RISEN LORD APPEARS

The silence of the grave could not hold the Word of Life. Jesus had risen, just as He said. But the glory of the resurrection was not merely in the empty tomb—it was in what happened immediately after.

Before He Continued Appearing — He Ascended to the Father

When Jesus first appeared to Mary Magdalene, He said something deeply profound:

" "But Christ came as High Priest of the good things to come, with the greater and more perfect tabernacle not made with hands, that is, not of this creation. Not with the blood of goats and calves, but with His own blood He entered the Most Holy Place once for all, having obtained eternal redemption."

Hebrews 9:11-12 NKJV

This moment reveals something often overlooked Jesus not yet glorified in heaven, had risen in bodily form. But there was a heavenly presentation yet to be fulfilled, according to the pattern laid out in the Old Testament, the High Priest, after offering the blood of atonement, had to enter the Holy of Holies to present that blood before God on behalf of the people (Leviticus 16).

Jesus, our Great High Priest, had carried out the sacrifice on the cross. Now, He needed to ascend to the true Holy of Holies in heaven and present His own blood before the throne of the Father.

This is why Jesus told Mary not to hold on to Him. The mission was not yet complete. He was ascending to complete the atonement, glorified by the Father, and to officially inaugurate the New Covenant.

His Glorification Marked the Turning Point:

Once glorified (John 17:5), Jesus would return and appear to His disciples—this time allowing them to touch Him, speak with Him, and even eat with Him. The shift in His interactions shows the change that had occurred in heaven. The work finished, the offering accepted, and now He was appearing not just as the crucified Savior, but as the risen, glorified Lord.

This glorification also fulfilled Jesus 'own prayer"And now, O Father, glorify Me together with Yourself, with the glory which I had with You before the world was." (John 17:5)

Mary Magdalene — The First to See the Risen Lord (John 20:11–18)

After His glorification, Jesus reappeared to Mary Magdalene, who had still been near the tomb, weeping. Her love for Him kept her close—even when others had left. In her grief, she did not recognize Him at first, mistaking Him for the gardener.

But then He said her name— "Mary." And at the sound of her name, she knew.

"Rabboni!" (which means Teacher)

Jesus had chosen Mary Magdalene, a woman once bound by seven demons (Luke 8:2), to be the first witness of His resurrection. Her deep affection and devotion were honored. She was sent with the greatest message ever spoken:

"Go to My brethren and say to them..." (John 20:17)

This speaks to the transforming grace of God—where once she was cast aside by society, now she was sent as the first herald of the resurrection.

The Other Women — "Rejoice!" (Matthew 28:9-10)

"And as they went to tell His disciples, behold, Jesus met them, saying, "Rejoice!" So, they came and held Him by the feet and worshiped Him. Then Jesus said to them, "Do not be afraid. Go and tell My brethren to go to Galilee, and there they will see Me.""

— Matthew 28:9-10 NKJV

As Mary ran to tell the disciples, Jesus also appeared to the other women who had come with spices to anoint His body. He met them along the way and greeted them with one word:

"Rejoice!"

They fell at His feet and worshiped Him. This moment was not just about reassurance—it was a command to enter the joy of His resurrection. Grief had turned to worship. Sorrow swallowed by joy.

Jesus instructed them to tell the disciples to meet Him in Galilee.

Peter — A Private Restoration (Luke 24:34; 1 Corinthians 15:5)

Sometime later that day, Jesus appeared privately to Peter. Though Scripture does not give us details of what happened, we can imagine the weight of that moment. Peter, who had denied Him three times, was now face to face with the One he had failed. This was not a moment of rebuke, but of restoration. The Shepherd had come to recover His wounded sheep.

The Road to Emmaus — Eyes Opened in the Breaking of Bread (Luke 24:13–35)

Two of His followers were walking to the village of Emmaus, heartbroken and confused about all that had happened. Jesus drew near, but their eyes were restrained. He opened the Scriptures to them, explaining how the Messiah must suffer and then enter His glory—beginning with Moses and the Prophets. Still, they did not recognize Him.

But when He broke the bread…

"Their eyes were opened, and they knew Him; and He vanished from their sight." (Luke 24:31)

This is a powerful picture: Jesus is revealed when the Word is opened, and the Bread of Life is broken. Their hearts had burned within them as He spoke—and now, they raced back to Jerusalem to share the news.

The Disciples (Without Thomas) — Behind Locked Doors (John 20:19–23)

That evening, the disciples gathered behind locked doors for fear of the Jews. Suddenly, Jesus appeared among them, saying:

"Peace be with you."

He showed them His hands and side. Their sorrow turned to gladness. Then He breathed on them, and said:

"Receive the Holy Spirit."

This was a foreshadowing of Pentecost—the breath of new life, a new covenant, and a new commission. They were bone again of the Spirit now awaiting Pentecost to be baptized in the Spirit and to receive power from on high.

The Disciples (With Thomas) — "My Lord and My God!" (John 20:24–29)

Eight days later, Jesus appeared again—this time, Thomas was present. The disciple who doubted offered the very evidence he asked for.

"Reach your finger here and look at My hands; and reach your hand here and put it into My side."

"Do not be unbelieving but believing."

Thomas, overwhelmed, cried:

"My Lord and my God!"

Jesus affirmed the faith of all who would believe without seeing:

"Blessed are those who have not seen and yet have believed."

The Seven Disciples at the Sea of Galilee — "Do You Love Me?" (John 21:1–23)

Later, Jesus appeared to seven of the disciples by the Sea of Galilee (Tiberias). Peter had said, "I am going fishing," unsure of what came next. They toiled all night and caught nothing—until Jesus, standing on the shore, called out:

"Cast the net on the right side of the boat..."

They caught 153 large fish, yet the net was not torn. This miraculous catch mirrored their original calling and was a reminder that apart from Him, they could do nothing. On the shore, Jesus had already prepared breakfast. After they ate, He turned to Peter, who had denied Him three times, and asked him three times:

"Do you love Me?"

With each affirmation, Jesus replied:

"Feed My lambs... Tend My sheep... Feed My sheep."

This moment was not just restoration—it was recommissioning. Jesus was preparing Peter to be

a shepherd of His flock, a pillar in the early Church.

The Mountain in Galilee — The Great Commission (Matthew 28:16–20)

Then, Jesus appeared to the eleven disciples on a mountain in Galilee, as He had instructed through the women.

Some worshiped; others still doubted. But Jesus came near and declared:

"All authority has been given to Me in heaven and on earth."

He then gave them what we now call the Great Commission:

"Go therefore and make disciples of all the nations, baptizing them in the name of the Father and of the Son and of the Holy Spirit, teaching them to observe all things that I have commanded you."

And His promise to them—and to us:

"And lo, I am with you always, even to the end of the age."

The Appearance to Over 500 at Once (1 Corinthians 15:6)

Paul records that Jesus appeared to over 500 brethren at once, many of whom were still alive at the time Paul wrote to the Corinthians. This mass appearance served as undeniable proof of the resurrection, proving a strong eyewitness testimony across the early Church.

James the Lord's Brother (1 Corinthians 15:7)

Jesus also appeared specifically to James, His half-brother. James had previously been a skeptic (John 7:5), but after this appearance, he became a pillar of the Jerusalem church (Galatians 1:19). His encounter with the risen Christ transformed doubt into devoted leadership.

The Ascension — "You Shall Be Witnesses" (Acts 1:3–11)

After appearing to His disciples over forty days, speaking of the kingdom of God and showing many infallible proofs, Jesus led them out to the Mount of Olives. There He gave His final instruction:

"You shall receive power when the Holy Spirit has come upon you; and you shall be witnesses to Me... to the end of the earth."

Then, as they watched, He was taken up, and a cloud received Him out of their sight.

Two angels stood by and said:

"This same Jesus, who was taken up from you into heaven, will

so come in like manner..."

Reflection: The Risen Lord, the Glorified Christ

These appearances were not just proof of life—they were invitations to transformation. Jesus met His followers in their fear, doubt, confusion, and failure—and He restored, commissioned, and empowered them. The resurrection was not the end of the story—it was the beginning of the Church's mission.

A Call to Respond: He Is Risen, Just as He Said

The appearances of Jesus after His resurrection were not random—they were intentional, purposeful, and deeply personal. He appeared to Mary to honor love. He appeared to Peter to restore the broken. He revealed Himself to doubters like Thomas, to the discouraged on the road to Emmaus, to the disciples in hiding, to the multitudes, and even to His once-skeptical brother. These were not just moments in history. They are divine reminders that Jesus meets us where we are—and then calls us to where He is.

He did not rise to merely be admired—He rose to be followed. He rose to call the fearful into boldness, the hopeless into purpose, and the sinful into grace. If you have not yet surrendered your life to the risen Christ, now is the time. This same Jesus who appeared to many is alive today, offering you forgiveness, eternal life, and intimate fellowship with the Father. If you have known Him but grown cold, let His voice rekindle your heart as it did for Peter: "Do you love Me?"

Prayer of Response:

Lord Jesus,

You are the risen Savior, the One who conquered death and lives forevermore.

You revealed Yourself with tenderness, with power, and with purpose.

You met Mary in her sorrow, Peter in his failure, Thomas in his doubt, and the disciples in their fear.

Meet me now, Lord.

You died for my sins and rose again on the third day. Forgive me, cleanse me, and make me new.

I surrender to You as my Savior and Lord.

Teach me to follow You with all my heart, to hear Your voice, and to fulfill the calling You have placed on my life. Let me live in the power of Your resurrection OH LORD. Amen.

CHAPTER 18: THREE COMMISSIONS AND THE REFORMATION OF PETER

After rising from the dead, Jesus did not at once ascend to the Father and remain hidden from His disciples. Instead, He spent forty days appearing to them, teaching, confirming their faith, and preparing them for the mission ahead. The number forty means probation not only was He teaching the disciples kingdom matters but He was also testing their obedience. These were not ordinary appearances—they were moments of divine instruction, filled with urgency, authority, and a call to carry the torch of truth into a mysterious world filled with evil and lawlessness.

The Gospels records three distinct commissions from the risen Christ. Each took place at a specific moment, to a specific audience, and each carried layers of meaning, fulfillment, and prophetic significance

The Commission in Luke 24 – Proclaiming Repentance and Forgiveness

Timing & Audience:

This occurred on the very evening of the resurrection. Jesus had just revealed Himself to the two disciples on the road to Emmaus and then appeared amid His disciples who gathered in fear and confusion in Jerusalem (Luke 24:36). His first words: "Peace to you." Then, He opened their minds to understand the Scriptures.

Theological Significance:

Jesus rooted the commission in prophecy:

"Thus, it is written, and thus it was necessary..." (Luke 24:46)

The preaching of repentance and forgiveness in His name is not a new concept—it was foretold. Isaiah 53 declared that the Servant would bear the iniquity of many. Joel prophesied that "whoever calls on the name of the Lord shall be saved." The resurrection confirmed this message.

End-Times Connection:

The message begins in Jerusalem and extends outward (Acts 1:8). This progression parallels Jesus 'prophecy in Matthew 24:14:

"And this gospel of the kingdom will be preached in all the world as a witness to all the nations, and then the end will come."

The end cannot come until the message of repentance reaches every nation. This makes the first commission not just a message—but a countdown to the fulfillment of time.

The Commission in Mark 16 – Preaching with Power and Signs

Timing & Audience:

Given after several appearances, this commission summarizes His instruction during the 40 days before the ascension. Jesus now speaks to them not as scattered sheep but as a prepared remnant.

"Go into all the world and preach the gospel to every creature." (Mark 16:15)

Theological Significance:

This commission affirms the universal scope of the Gospel. The phrase "every creature" (Greek: pasa ktisis) emphasizes that no person, no group, no region is excluded.

He also promises signs that would go upon with those who believe—casting out demons, speaking in new tongues, healing the sick. These are not random manifestations but confirmations of His power.

"how shall we escape if we neglect so great a salvation, which at the first began to be spoken by the Lord, and was confirmed to us by those who heard Him, God also bearing

witness both with signs and wonders, with various miracles, and gifts of the Holy Spirit, according to His own will?"

— Hebrews 2:3-4 NKJV

End-Times Connection:

This lines up with Jesus 'words in Mark 13:10:

"And the gospel must first be preached to all the nations."

The emphasis is on movement, action, and urgency. In Revelation 14:6, we see an angel flying in mid-heaven with an "everlasting gospel to preach to those who dwell on the earth—to every nation, tribe, tongue, and people." The church is the forerunner of that global declaration.

The Commission in Matthew 28 – Discipling the Nations Under the

Authority of the King

Timing & Audience:

This occurred later in Galilee, as Jesus had instructed through the women after His resurrection. The location itself is significant—Galilee of the Gentiles (Isaiah 9:1), where Jesus began His public ministry, now becomes the launch point of the global mission.

"All authority has been given to Me in heaven and on earth." (Matthew 28:18)

Theological Significance:

Here, Jesus does not simply send them—He sends them with all authority. The Great Commission is not only a mandate but a kingdom decree. Making disciples of all nations,

baptizing them and teaching them to observe all things means more than conversion—it is about transformation.

End-Times Connection:

This aligns perfectly with the parable of the wise and foolish virgins (Matthew 25), the parable of the talents, and the judgment of the nations. Jesus is not just calling us to be ready but to be fruitful and faithful in the work while we wait. Jesus did not give these commissions lightly.

Each one builds upon the other—from preaching repentance to bold proclamation with signs, to teaching and discipling under His authority. Together, they form the foundation of the Church's mission in this present age. They are also part of the prophetic sequence leading to the end. The more the Gospel advances, the closer we draw to His return. Every disciple who shares the message, every church that teaches His commands, every nation that hears the name of Jesus— moves us one step to the trump sound.

The Restoration of Peter – By the Charcoal Fire (John 21)

Setting the Scene:

The disciples, still processing the appearances of Jesus in Jerusalem, had returned to Galilee— just as Jesus instructed. There, some of them went fishing. After a fruitless night, they heard a familiar voice call from the shore:

"Children, have you any food?" (John 21:5)

They had caught nothing—until Jesus told them to cast the net on the right side of the boat. Suddenly, they caught 153 large fish, and the net did not break. The disciple whom Jesus loved (John) recognized Him first:

"It is the Lord!"

The Significance of the Fire:

When they reached the shore, Jesus had already prepared a charcoal fire with fish and bread (John 21:9). This detail is not random—the only other place "charcoal fire" (Greek: anthrakia) appears in Scripture is in John 18:18, where Peter denied Jesus three times.

Now, Jesus is about to undo Peter's shame around a new charcoal fire.

The Threefold Question: "Do You Love Me?"

Jesus turns to Peter and asks not once, but three times:

"Simon, son of Jonah, do you love Me?"

Peter responds each time, growing more sorrowful with each question. Jesus responds with a commission each time:

- Feed My lambs.
- Tend My sheep.
- Feed My sheep.

Why three times? It was a prophetic and emotional reversal of Peter's three denials. Jesus was not rubbing salt into the wound—He was healing it with truth and grace.

This was not just forgiveness—it was restoration and recommissioning. Jesus did not just want Peter back as a follower—He was reinstating him as a shepherd, a leader, a foundational apostle.

Prophetic Weight and End-Times Insight:

Jesus ends this moment by telling Peter:

"When you were younger, you girded yourself and walked where you wished; but when you are old, you will stretch out your hands…" (John 21:18)

This was a prophecy of Peter's future martyrdom—a powerful call to endurance and faithfulness unto death. Just as Peter would feed Jesus 'sheep, we are to shepherd one another in truth, especially as the end draws near. The same restored Peter who would later write:

"The end of all things is at hand; therefore, be serious and watchful in your prayers." (1 Peter 4:7)

Reflection and Invitation:

Peter denied Jesus when fear overwhelmed him. But Jesus did not discard him. He pursued him. Friend, you might have denied Him—not with words, but with your lifestyle, your compromises, your silence when you should have spoken. But the same Jesus who restored Peter by the fire wants to restore you.

Do you love Him?

That is the question He still asks today.

Not, did you fail Me?

Not, did you promise and fall again? But—Do you love Me?

Let the fire of His grace burn away your shame. Let His voice restore your identity. Let His commission send you out—not with guilt, but with glory.

The Greek Behind the Words:

- Jesus asked: "Do you agapaō Me?"

(ἀγαπάω – the highest form of love: sacrificial, unconditional, divine.)

- Peter responded: "Yes, Lord, you know that I phileō You."

(φιλέω – a love of friendship, affection, deep personal connection.)

Peter, still wounded by his threefold denial, could no longer boast. He could not bring himself to say he loved Jesus with the agapē kind of love—not after what he had done. But he was honest: "Lord, I phileō You—I love You as a friend."

Jesus asked again—and Peter answered the same.

Then the third time, Jesus met Peter at his level, asking:

"Simon, son of Jonah, do you phileō Me?"

This time Peter was grieved. Jesus had stepped into Peter's brokenness, asking not for what Peter wished he could offer, but for what he truly could.

A Love That Restores:

Three times Peter denied Jesus.

Three times Jesus asked, "Do you love Me?" Three times Jesus responded with commission:

"Feed My lambs... Tend My sheep... Feed My sheep."

This was not a scolding—it was a divine reinstatement.

Jesus was not only restoring Peter's role as a disciple—He was revealing the heart of God:

a Shepherd who lifts the fallen, a Savior who meets us in our lowest moment and calls us higher.

Reflection: From Phileō to Agapē:

Peter began this journey thinking he would die for Jesus. But his strength failed.

Now, humbled and healed, Peter's journey truly begins—not with pride, but with surrendered love.

In time, Peter would indeed grow from phileō to agapē.

He would eventually lay down his life for the Lord he once denied.

So, the question echoes today…

"Do you love Me?"

Not, do you have a perfect record? Not, are you strong enough?

But—do you love Me—even in your weakness?

A Prayer of Response:

Lord Jesus, I may not love You perfectly, but I do love You. Meet me where I am—and lead me into deeper love.

Make me faithful. Restore what is broken. And use me, like Peter, to feed Your sheep. Amen.

CHAPTER 19: THE ASCENSION AND THE PROMISED HOLY SPIRIT

The risen Lord had shown Himself alive by many infallible proofs over the span of forty days (Acts 1:3), speaking to His disciples of the things about the kingdom of God. He had restored the

broken, opened the Scriptures, and rekindled the flame of faith. But now the time had come for Him to return to the Father—to ascend in glory, and to send the Holy Spirit to empower the Church.

The Ascension: A Heavenly Departure with Earthly Significance

"Now when He had spoken these things, while they watched, He was taken up, and a cloud received Him out of their sight."

—Acts 1:9 (NKJV)

Jesus led His disciples as far as Bethany, lifted His hands, and blessed them (Luke 24:50). In that final earthly moment with them, He was carried up into heaven—visibly, bodily, gloriously. This was no disappearance or vision—it was a literal ascension, and they stood gazing upward until two angels appeared and spoke:

"Men of Galilee, why do you stand gazing up into heaven? This same Jesus, who was taken up from you into heaven, will so come in like manner..."

—Acts 1:11

This statement confirmed two vital truths: His exaltation was real, and His return will be just as real. The ascension was not the end—it was the transition from the earthly ministry of Jesus to His heavenly ministry as High Priest, Intercessor, and soon-returning King.

The Promise of the Father:

Before ascending, Jesus gave His disciples a clear instruction:

"Behold, I send the Promise of My Father upon you; but tarry in the city of Jerusalem until you are endued with power from on high."

— Luke 24:49

"You shall receive power when the Holy Spirit has come upon you; and you shall be witnesses to Me..."

—Acts 1:8

This "Promise of the Father" was the Holy Spirit—the very Spirit that had empowered Jesus in His earthly ministry, now to be poured out upon the Church. The same Spirit who hovered over the waters at creation, who filled the prophets, who raised Jesus from the dead, would now rest upon every believer and ignite a global mission.

Fulfilled Prophecy, Unstoppable Mission

The ascension of Jesus fulfilled ancient prophecy:

- Psalm 68:18 "–You have ascended on high; you have led captivity captive; You have received gifts among men…"
- Daniel 7:13–14 "–One like the Son of Man… came with the clouds of heaven… and to

Him was given dominion and glory and a kingdom…"

From heaven, Jesus would soon send the Holy Spirit on the Day of Pentecost (Acts 2), ushering in the birth of the Church and launching the age of the Spirit. His disciples—once fearful and scattered—would now be bold witnesses unto the ends of the earth.

Final Reflection: From the Cross to the Cloud

From His humble birth to His triumphant resurrection, from His cross to the cloud that received Him, Jesus fulfilled every word the Father had spoken. He was the Lamb who was slain, the Servant who suffered, the Savior who rose, and the King who ascended. And yet—His story is not over.

He is coming again.

The signs He gave us in Matthew 24 and Luke 21 are increasing in frequency and intensity. The

fig tree is budding. The earth groans. The Spirit still calls. And the Lord is even at the door.

But until He comes, we are not left powerless.

"Lo, I am with you always, even to the end of the age."

— Matthew 28:20

Through the indwelling Spirit, Jesus is in us and through the outpouring of the Holy Spirit, Jesus is Empowering us. Sending us. Loving through us. The ascension did not remove His presence— it multiplied it.

A Final Call

If you have journeyed through this book and your heart has been stirred, do not let it stop at emotion. Let it move you to decision.

If you have never given your life to Jesus Christ, now is the time. He is not just a historical figure—He is the risen, ascended Lord who will return. His blood was shed for your sins. His resurrection guarantees your eternal life. His Spirit waits to dwell within you.

Pray this:

Lord Jesus, I believe you are the Son of God. I believe you died for my sins and rose again. I repent of my sins and ask You to forgive me. I receive You now as my Savior and my Lord. Fill me with Your Spirit. Lead me and use me until the day You return. Amen.

And if you are already born again—be filled afresh with the Holy Spirit. Be bold. Be watchful. Be faithful. The King of Kings and the Lord of Lords is at hand even at the door.

Pentecost — The Fire Fell, and the Church Was Born:

They waited as Jesus commanded. In the upper room, about 120 believers gathered (Acts 1:15), praying, worshipping, and expecting the Promise of the Father. They did not know how it would come, but they believed He would fulfill His Word.

Then suddenly—on the Day of Pentecost, fifty days after the resurrection, ten days after the ascension—Heaven moved.

"When the Day of Pentecost had fully come, they were all with one accord in one place. And suddenly there came a sound from heaven, as of a rushing mighty wind, and it filled the whole house where they were sitting. Then there appeared to them divided tongues, as of fire, and one sat upon each of them. And they were all filled with the Holy Spirit and began to speak with other tongues, as the Spirit gave them

utterance."

—Acts 2:1-4 NKJV

The Holy Spirit was no longer just upon select prophets or kings. He now filled men and women, young and old, weak, and strong. This was the birth of the Church—the indwelling power of God now in every believer. Just as the veil had been torn in the temple, now the Spirit no longer dwelled in a building of stone, but in living temples—our hearts (1 Corinthians 6:19).

The Transformed Peter:

And then, Peter stood up. The same Peter who had denied Jesus three times. The same Peter who had wept bitterly in shame. But something had changed. Peter was now filled with the Holy Spirit. He lifted his voice and declared boldly to the multitudes, quoting Joel's prophecy and proclaiming Jesus as the risen Messiah (Acts 2:14–36). No longer fearful, Peter preached with clarity and conviction—and 3,000 souls were saved that day (Acts 2:41). This was not just revival—it was regeneration. The Spirit who raised Christ from the dead now lived in Peter, and through him, Christ's power and message thundered into the world. And it has not stopped since.

From Pentecost to the Present:

The fire that fell at Pentecost was not only for the early Church. It was for every generation until the Lord returns.

"For the promise is to you and to your children, and to all who

are afar off, as many as the Lord our God will call."

—Acts 2:39

That includes you. The same Spirit is still being poured out. The same power is still manifesting miracles, sign and wonders and transforming souls. And the same Jesus is still coming back not as the Son of God but highly elevated to His magnificent King of Kings and Lord of Lords ready for battle and to rule His Kingdom with blessing, and honor, and glory, and power.

The signs He gave us are being fulfilled in our very days. The shaking of nations. The cry for peace and safety. The increase of wickedness. The preaching of the gospel to all nations. The fig tree has blossomed, and the Bridegroom is at the door.

Final Reflection: There Is Still Hope

Jesus has ascended—but He is not absent. He has risen—but He is not distant. He has poured out His Spirit—and He has promised to return.

This book is not just a recounting of history. It is a call to decision.

- If you have felt dry—seek the fullness of the Holy Spirit.
- If you have strayed—return to your first love.
- If you have doubted—look again at the empty tomb.
- If you have grown weary—remember the promise of His coming.

Peter was restored. Mary was honored. Thomas was assured. You are not beyond reach. Let the fire of Pentecost ignite your heart again. Let the cross break your pride. Let the empty tomb breathe hope into your soul. Let the ascension lift your eyes upward. And let the promise of His return keep your heart watching.

"Even so, come, Lord Jesus."

— Revelation 22 :20

Until He comes, we are His voice. His hands. His light. His ambassadors.

The story is not over.

It is just the beginning.

A Personal Letter to You, the Reader

Dear Beloved,

As I bring this book to its final words, I find myself overwhelmed—not just with the completion of these pages, but with the deep, indescribable weight of His rejection, His weeping, His persecution, His suffering, His crucifiction, His death and His resurrection, I have had the privilege to write not withholding my own experience sorrow and weeping but yet rejoicing in the hope of His return

There were moments while writing—especially when recounting the suffering of Jesus, His scourging, the betrayal, the tears in Gethsemane, the thorns, the nails, the brutal beating—that I had to stop and weep. It was not just sorrow. It was a holy grief, a piercing awareness of what He endured—for me, for you, for the world.

I was not just telling a story—I was meeting the heart of the Savior. I saw the blood-soaked mercy of the King who left His crown and chose the cross. I heard the echo of His cry, "Father, forgive them," and realized it was for all of us. Even now, as I write this letter, I feel the same trembling reverence I felt during those moments.

To know Jesus is to be undone by His love, mercy, and goodness. His wounds speak louder than words. His silence before His accusers is more powerful than the roar of armies. His cross breaks our pride, and His resurrection lifts us out of our graves. Even as the writer, I cannot come out of this journey unchanged. And I pray with all my heart—you have not either.

This is more than a story or history. It is holy reality.

This is more than theology or doctrine. It is the heartbeat of God.

This is not just about what Jesus did. It is about who He is—right now.

Alive. Exalted. Soon returning.

If you are already walking with Him, may this draw you closer than ever. If you have grown cold, may it rekindle your fire.

If you have never surrendered to Him—please do not turn away. He is calling you even now. He took the beating for your healing.

He bore the shame for your acceptance.

He wore the thorns so you could wear a crown. He died so you could live.

This book has broken me in the best way.

And I pray it has broken something in you too—not to destroy, but to make room for something eternal to be born.

Thank you for walking this road to Calvary with me.

Let us live with eyes fixed on the One who is coming again.

With love, trembling reverence, and hope,

peter lengwe

A fellow follower, broken and made whole by His grace.

If as you read this, your heart has been stirred—if you have felt a tug, a whisper, a warmth, or even tears—you are not alone. That is Jesus. He is calling you. Not to religion. Not to rules. But to relationship—a restored, eternal relationship with the God who made you and died to save you.

Do not wait another day. Open your heart. He is closer than you think.

A Simple Prayer of Surrender:

Pray this with all your heart:

Lord Jesus,

I believe you are the Son of God.

I believe you died on the cross for my sins. I believe you rose from the dead.

I confess that I am a sinner, and I ask You to forgive me.

Wash me with Your blood.

I surrender my life to You—my heart, my soul, my past, my future. Come into my life and be my Lord and Savior.

Fill me with Your Holy Spirit.

Help me to live for You from this day forward.

Thank You for loving me, for saving me, and for giving me eternal life.

In the name of Jesus, Amen.

If you prayed that prayer sincerely, welcome home. You are now a child of God. The journey does not end here—it is just beginning. Open the Word. Seek Him daily. Find a Bible-believing community. And never forget—the One who saved you is coming back for you.

APPENDIX A-P

Appendix A: Passion Week Timeline

Understanding Time in the Jewish Calendar

- The Jewish day begins at sunset (around 6:00 PM) and ends at the next day's sunset.
- This differs from the Gregorian calendar, where the day begins and ends at midnight.
- Recognizing this distinction is key to correctly understanding the timeline of Jesus 'final days, including His crucifixion, burial, and resurrection.

Passion Week Day-by-Day Timeline

Jewish Day	Approx. Gregorian Day	Key Events
Nisan 8 (Evening)	Saturday evening	Jesus arrives in Bethany (John 12:1)

Nisan 9 (Day)	Sunday	Supper at Simon the leper's house; Mary anoints Jesus for burial (Mark 14:3)
Nisan 10 (Day)	Monday	Triumphal Entry into Jerusalem (Matthew 21:11)
Nisan 11 (Day)	Tuesday	Jesus weeps over Jerusalem; Cleanses the Temple
Nisan 12 (Day)	Wednesday	Teaching in the Temple; confrontation with religious leaders
Nisan 13 (Day)	Thursday	Judas agrees to betray Jesus (Mark 14:10-11); Preparation for Passover begins
Nisan 14 (Evening)	Thursday evening	Last Supper (Luke 22); Jesus prays in Gethsemane
Nisan 14 (Day)	Friday (daytime)	Jesus is tried, crucified, and buried before sunset
Nisan 15 (High Sabbath)	Friday sunset Saturday	First night and day in the tomb (Feast of Unleavened Bread begins)
Nisan 16 (Second Night)	Saturday (night)	Second night in the tomb
Nisan 17 (Third Night)	Saturday after sunset	Resurrection occurs after Sabbath sunset
Nisan 17 (Day)	Sunday	Mary Magdalene sees the risen Lord (John 20:1

Key Theological Correction:

- Jesus said, "Just as Jonah was three days and three nights in the belly of the great fish…" (Matthew 12:40).
- A Friday crucifixion does not allow for three full days and three nights.
- The correct timeline—Wednesday crucifixion before Passover (High Sabbath) and Saturday evening resurrection—fulfills this prophecy precisely.

Why This Matters

Understanding the actual Passion Week timeline:

- Restores biblical accuracy
- Affirms Jesus' own prophetic words
- Unmasks traditions that have blurred the truth (e.g., Friday crucifixion taught by religious institutions)
- Deepens your appreciation for the precision of God's plan of redemption

Appendix B: Greek Word Studies and Their Significance

Understanding the original Greek brings clarity, depth, and intensity to the events surrounding the suffering, death, and resurrection of Jesus. These words are not mere translations—they are revelations.

1. Agapáō (ἀγαπάω) vs. Phileō (φιλέω)

Passage: John 21:15–17 Context: Jesus restores Peter.

- Agapáō – divine, unconditional, sacrificial love.
- Phileō – brotherly, affectionate, emotional love.

Jesus asked Peter if he loved Him more than the others. Peter replied, "Yes, Lord, you know I love (phileō) You." On the third question, Jesus used Peter's word (phileō).

This shift shows Jesus' meeting Peter where he was emotionally, then raising him up again in grace.

Insight: Jesus gently restores Peter from shame, using language that first confronts and then embraces. This exchange pierces the heart of every follower who has ever failed Him.

2. Tetelestai (Τετέλεσται)

Passage: John 19:30

Translation: "It is finished."

This is a legal and financial term meaning:

"Paid in full. The debt is cancelled."

Insight: Jesus did not merely die—He fulfilled the righteous requirement of the law and paid the price for sin. Nothing remains to be done to earn salvation.

3. Parousía (παρουσία)

Passage: Matthew 24:3

Translation: "What will be the sign of Your coming (parousía)?"

- Parousía means presence, arrival, or royal visitation.
- In the New Testament, it refers to Jesus 'second coming in glory and judgment.

Insight: His first coming was in humility. His second will be in power. The word parousía carried deep royal connotations in the Greek world—used when kings entered a city. Jesus will return, not as a suffering servant, but as a conquering King.

4. Skēnē (σκηνή)

Passage: John 1:14

Translation: "And the Word became flesh and dwelt (skēnē) among us."

- Skēnē – to tabernacle, to pitch a tent.
  Used of God's dwelling in the wilderness tabernacle.

Insight: Jesus is the fulfillment of the tabernacle. God's presence was no longer behind a veil— He came among us in Jesus and now lives within believers through the Holy Spirit.

5. Anástasis (ἀνάστασις)

Passage: John 11:25

Translation: "I am the resurrection (anástasis) and the life."

- Anástasis – a rising again, resurrection from death.

Insight: Resurrection was not just something Jesus did—it is who He is. Through His anástasis, He conquered death once for all.

6. Blasphemía (βλασφημία)

Passage: Matthew 26:65

Translation: "He has uttered blasphemy!"

- Blasphemía – to slander, speak evil of God.

Insight: Jesus was accused of blasphemy for telling the truth about His divinity. What man called blasphemy, heaven called truth.

7. Dikaiōō (δικαιόω)

Passage: Romans 5:1

Translation: "Therefore, having been justified (dikaiōō) by faith…"

- Dikaiōō – to declare righteous, to acquit from guilt.

Insight: Through the cross and resurrection, Jesus did not just forgive our sin—He declared us righteous before the Father. This is legal justification, not mere pardon.

These words are more than linguistic detail—they are theological cornerstones of the Gospel.

Appendix C: Prophecies Fulfilled During Passion Week

The final week of Jesus Christ's life is saturated with prophetic fulfillment. These were not random events—they were ordained by God, foretold in Scripture, and fulfilled down to the smallest detail. They testify to the divine authorship of the Bible and the identity of Jesus as the promised Messiah.

1. Triumphal Entry – Zechariah 9:9

Prophecy:

"Rejoice greatly, O daughter of Zion... your king comes to you... lowly and riding upon a donkey."

— Zechariah 9:9

Fulfilled:

"Behold, your King is coming... sitting on a donkey's colt." – Matthew 21:5

Insight: Jesus entered Jerusalem as the humble King, not a political conqueror. The manner of His entry—on a donkey—declared peace, not war.

2. Betrayed for 30 Pieces of Silver – Zechariah 11:12–13

Prophecy:

"So, they weighed for my price thirty pieces of silver... and cast them to the potter in the house of the Lord."

— Zechariah 11:12–13

Fulfilled:

"They counted out to him thirty pieces of silver... and the chief priests... bought with them the potter's field."

— Matthew 26:15; 27:3–10

Insight: Judas 'betrayal price and the purchase of the potter's field fulfilled an obscure prophecy with pinpoint accuracy.

3. Silent Before His Accusers – Isaiah 53:7

Prophecy:

"He was oppressed... yet He opened not His mouth." – Isaiah 53:7

Fulfilled:

"But Jesus remained silent and gave no answer." – Mark 14:61; Matthew 27:12–14

Insight: The Lamb of God, though unjustly accused, did not defend Himself—He was willingly offering Himself as a sacrifice.

4. Scourged and Bruised – Isaiah 53:5

Prophecy:

"He was wounded for our transgressions... and by His stripes we are healed."

— Isaiah 53:5

Fulfilled:

"Then he released Barabbas... and scourged Jesus." – Matthew 27:26

Insight: Roman scourging was brutal, yet every stripe fulfilled prophecy—and bought our healing.

5. Garments Divided and Lots Cast – Psalm 22:18

Prophecy:

"They divide My garments among them, and for My clothing they cast

lots."

— Psalm 22:18

Fulfilled:

"They divided His garments... and cast lots." – John 19:23–24

Insight: Even the Roman soldiers unknowingly fulfilled prophecy, as they gambled over His seamless robe.

6. Given Gall and Vinegar – Psalm 69:21

Prophecy:

"They gave Me gall for My food, and for My thirst they gave Me vinegar to drink."

— Psalm 69:21

Fulfilled:

"They gave Him sour wine mingled with gall to drink." – Matthew 27:34

Insight: The bitterness He drank was not just physical—it symbolized the cup of wrath He bore for us.

7. Pierced Hands and Feet – Psalm 22:16; Zechariah 12:10

Prophecy:

"They pierced My hands and My feet."

"They will look on Me whom they pierced." – Psalm 22:16; Zechariah 12:10

Fulfilled:

"When they came to Jesus... they did not break His legs... but one of the soldiers pierced His side with a spear."

– John 19:33–37

Insight: Crucifixion, unknown in David's day, centuries before it was used.

8. Not One Bone Broken – Exodus 12:46; Psalm 34:20

Prophecy:

"Not one of His bones shall be broken."

Psalm 34:20; Exodus 12:46 (about the Passover lamb)

Fulfilled:

"They broke the legs of the others... but when they came to Jesus... they did not break His legs."

—John 19:33, 36

Insight: Jesus, the true Passover Lamb, was protected from broken bones to fulfill the requirement of the sacrifice.

9. Buried with the Rich – Isaiah 53:9

Prophecy:

"They made His grave with the wicked—but with the rich at His death."

—Isaiah 53:9

Fulfilled:

"There came a rich man from Arimathea named Joseph... and laid [Jesus] in his own new tomb."

—Matthew 27:57–60

Insight: Though crucified as a criminal, Jesus was buried honorably fulfilling both justice and prophecy.

10. Raised from the Dead – Psalm 16:10; Hosea 6:2

Prophecy:

"You will not allow Your Holy One to see corruption."

"After two days He will revive us; on the third day He will raise us up."

— Psalm 16:10; Hosea 6:2

Fulfilled:

"He is not here, for He is risen as He said."

— Matthew 28:6

Insight: The resurrection was not a surprise—it was a divine appointment.

These fulfilled prophecies are not simply prooftexts; they are divine fingerprints—evidence that God authored the salvation story before the foundation of the world.

Appendix D: Timeline of Passion Week Events

To better understand the flow and depth of the final week of Jesus 'life, we must align the Gospel accounts with the Jewish calendar—which begins days at sunset, not midnight—and distinguish High Sabbaths (feast day Sabbaths) from regular weekly Sabbaths.

This revised timeline offers a biblically and historically exact view of Passion Week, clearing up misconceptions—especially the idea of a Friday crucifixion, which contradicts Jesus 'own words about being in the heart of the earth for "three days and three nights" (Matthew 12:40).

Day 1 – The Triumphal Entry

Date: Saturday evening–Sunday (Nisan 10)

Key Event: Jesus rides into Jerusalem on a donkey

Scripture: Matthew 21:1–11; Mark 11:1–11; Luke 19:28–44; John 12:12–15

Fulfills Zechariah 9:9

Day 2 – Cleansing the Temple

Date: Sunday evening–Monday (Nisan 11) Key Event: Jesus clears the temple courts

Scripture: Matthew 21:12–17; Mark 11:15–19; Luke 19:45–48

Day 3 – Teaching & Confrontation

Date: Monday evening–Tuesday (Nisan 12)

Key Event: Jesus teaches in the temple, rebukes Pharisees, weeps over Jerusalem Scripture: Matthew 21–23; Mark 11:20–33; Luke 20

Day 4 – Private Teachings (Mount of Olives)

Date: Tuesday evening–Wednesday (Nisan 13)

Key Event: Olivet Discourse—Jesus teaches about end times Scripture: Matthew 24–25; Mark 13; Luke 21

Likely the day Mary anointed Jesus (Mark 14:3–9)

Day 5 – Preparation Day for Passover

Date: Wednesday evening–Thursday (Nisan 14) Key Events:

- Jesus celebrates the Last Supper (evening beginning Nisan 14)
- Judas betrays Jesus
- Jesus is arrested, tried, scourged

- Jesus is crucified and buried before sunset
  Scripture: Matthew 26–27; Mark 14–15; Luke 22–23; John 13–19 This is the true day of crucifixion—not Friday
  He died before the High Sabbath began at sunset (John 19:31)

Day 6 – High Sabbath: First Day of Unleavened Bread

Date: Thursday sunset–Friday sunset (Nisan 15) Key Event: Jesus rests in the tomb

Scripture: Leviticus 23:6–7

No work was to be done—this was a feast-day Sabbath

Day 7 – Weekly Sabbath

Date: Friday sunset–Saturday sunset (Nisan 16) Key Event: Second day in the tomb

Scripture: Luke 23:56

Women rest according to the commandment

Resurrection – After Sunset (End of Weekly Sabbath)

Date: Saturday evening (start of Nisan 17)

Key Event: Jesus rises after three days and three nights

Scripture: Matthew 28:1–6; Mark 16:1–6; Luke 24:1–7; John 20:1–10 He is risen—before the women arrived at the tomb Sunday morning

Summary of "Three Days and Three Nights

Event	Timing (Jewish reckoning)
Burial Begins	Wed sunset (Nisan 14)
Night 1	Wed night
Day 1	Thurs (High Sabbath)
Night 2	Thurs night

Day 2	Friday
Night 3	Fri night
Day 3	Saturday (Weekly Sabbath)
Resurrection	After sunset, Sat night

Jesus rose after the third day had fully passed—not Sunday morning.

Appendix E: The Seven Sayings of Jesus on the Cross

Each word Jesus spoke from the cross was a window into His heart, revealing divine mercy, human suffering, fulfilled prophecy, and eternal hope. These are not random phrases, but deliberate declarations—each one layered with meaning and love.

1. "Father, forgive them, for they know not what they do."

— Luke 23:34

Even as He was nailed to the cross, Jesus interceded—not for Himself, but for His executioners. This was mercy in motion, echoing Isaiah 53:12, "He bore the sin of many and made intercession for the transgressors."

A call to forgive even our worst enemies.

2. "Truly, I say to you, today you will be with Me in Paradise."

Luke 23:43

Spoken to the repentant thief, this word offers hope to anyone who turns to Christ—even in their ultimate moments.

Salvation is not earned but received through faith in the Savior.

3. "Woman, behold your son… Behold your mother."

— John 19:26–27

Amid His suffering, Jesus made provision for His earthly mother. Even in agony, He showed deep compassion and honored His family.

4. "My God, My God, why have You forsaken Me?"

— Matthew 27:46; Mark 15:34

Quoting Psalm 22:1, Jesus expressed the spiritual agony of bearing the sin of the world. This was not a loss of faith, but a cry from the depths of substitution.

He was forsaken so we could be accepted.

5. "I thirst."

— John 19:28

Fulfilling Psalm 69:21, this shows Jesus 'true humanity. The Creator of water became thirsty for our sake.

He experienced thirst so we could drink the living water.

6. "It is finished."

— John 19:30

Greek: τετέλεσται (tetelestai) — a commercial term meaning "Paid in full." The debt of sin was settled. The work of redemption complete.

7. "Father, into Your hands I commit My Spirit."

— Luke 23:46

Jesus died not as a victim, but in total control, entrusting Himself to the Father. A model of trust in God, even unto death.

8. Reflection for the Reader

Every word on the cross speaks to our deepest need: forgiveness, salvation, acceptance, fulfillment, and relationship with the Father.

As you meditate on these sayings, let them soften your heart and draw you closer to the One who hung there for you.

Appendix F: Old Testament Prophecies Fulfilled During the Passion of Christ

The crucifixion and resurrection of Jesus were not accidents—they were the perfect fulfillment of God's eternal plan. Throughout His final hours, every action and moment fulfilled ancient Scripture, confirming His identity as the promised Messiah. This list highlights key Old Testament prophecies fulfilled during the Passion of Christ.

1. Betrayed by a Close Companion

Prophecy: "Even my close friend in whom I trusted, who ate my bread, has lifted his heel against me."

Psalm 41:9

Fulfillment: "Then Judas… went to the chief priests to betray Him." Matthew 26:14–16

2. Betrayed for Thirty Pieces of Silver

Prophecy: "So they weighed for my wages thirty pieces of silver." Zechariah 11:12

Fulfillment: "And they counted out to him thirty pieces of silver." Matthew 26:15

3. Money Thrown in God's House and Used for Potter's Field

Prophecy: "So I took the thirty pieces of silver… and threw them into the house of the Lord… for the potter."

Zechariah 11:13

Fulfillment: “They took the thirty pieces of silver… and bought with them the potter’s field.” Matthew 27:5–10

4. Silent Before His Accusers

Prophecy: “He was oppressed and afflicted, yet He did not open His mouth.” Isaiah 53:7

Fulfillment: “But He answered him not one word.”

Matthew 27:14

5. Beaten and Spat Upon

Prophecy: “I gave my back to those who strike, and my cheeks to those who pull out the beard; I hid not my face from disgrace and spitting.”

Isaiah 50:6

Fulfillment: “Then they spat in His face and struck Him.” Matthew 26:67

6. Pierced Hands and Feet

Prophecy: “They have pierced my hands and feet.” Psalm 22:16

Fulfillment: “They crucified Him…”

John 19:18

7. Casting Lots for His Garments

Prophecy: “They divide my garments among them, and for my clothing they cast lots.” Psalm 22:18

Fulfillment: “They cast lots to decide what each would take.”

Mark 15:24

8. Darkness at Noon

Prophecy: "And on that day… I will make the sun go down at noon and darken the earth in broad daylight."

Amos 8:9

Fulfillment: "From the sixth hour darkness fell over all the land until the ninth hour." Matthew 27:45

9. No Bones Broken

Prophecy: "Not one of His bones will be broken." Psalm 34:20; Exodus 12:46

Fulfillment: "They did not break His legs."

John 19:33

10. Pierced Side

Prophecy: "They will look on Me whom they have pierced." Zechariah 12:10

Fulfillment: "One of the soldiers pierced His side with a spear."

John 19:34–37

11. Buried with the Rich

Prophecy: "He was with a rich man in His death." Isaiah 53:9

Fulfillment: "A rich man from Arimathea named Joseph… laid Him in his own new tomb."

Matthew 27:57–60

12. Raised from the Dead

Prophecy: "You will not abandon my soul to Sheol or let Your holy one see corruption." Psalm 16:10

Fulfillment: "He is not here; He is risen just as He said."

Matthew 28:6

Reflection

These fulfilled prophecies are not only astonishing in accuracy but are a divine signature across centuries, pointing unmistakably to Jesus of Nazareth as the Christ, the Son of the Living God.

Let these truths ignite your faith and deepen your confidence in the unshakable Word of God.

Appendix G: Timeline of the Final Week of Jesus (Passion Week)

This timeline aligns the events of Jesus 'final week before the crucifixion, burial, and resurrection with the Jewish calendar and highlights the significance of each day. It also corrects common misconceptions—particularly the tradition of a Friday crucifixion—and presents a theologically and historically sound sequence based on Scripture.

Day 1 – Sunday (10th of Nisan): Triumphal Entry

Matthew 21:1–11; Mark 11:1–10; Luke 19:28–44; John 12:12–19

- Jesus enters Jerusalem riding on a donkey in fulfillment of Zechariah 9:9.
- The people cry, "Hosanna! Blessed is He who comes in the name of the Lord!"
- This marks the Lamb being presented for inspection (Exodus 12:3).

Day 2 – Monday (11th of Nisan): Cleansing the Temple

Matthew 21:12–17; Mark 11:15–19; Luke 19:45–48

- Jesus drives out money changers from the temple.
- He declares, "My house shall be called a house of prayer."
- Religious leaders begin plotting to destroy Him.

Day 3 – Tuesday (12th of Nisan): Day of Teaching and Prophecy

Matthew 21:23–24:2; Mark 11:27–13:2; Luke 20:1–21:4

- Jesus teaches in the temple and engages in confrontations with religious leaders.
- He weeps over Jerusalem and prophesies its destruction.
- The Olivet Discourse begins as He and His disciples leave the temple.
- Parables and prophetic warnings are given about the end times.

Day 4 – Tuesday Evening into Wednesday (13th of Nisan): Anointing & Betrayal

Matthew 26:1–16; Mark 14:1–11; Luke 22:1–6; John 12:1–8

- Jesus is anointed at Bethany in the house of Simon the leper.
- Judas goes to the chief priests to betray Jesus for thirty pieces of silver.
- This occurs two days before the Passover, aligning with Mark 14:1 and Matthew 26:2.

Day 5 – Wednesday (14th of Nisan): Preparation Day

Matthew 26:17–75; Mark 14:12–72; Luke 22:7–71; John 13–18

- Jesus celebrates the Last Supper with His disciples.

- He institutes the New Covenant in His blood.
- Jesus prays in Gethsemane and is arrested at night.
- He is taken to the high priest, where He is mocked, beaten, and denied by Peter.
- This is the day of preparation before the Passover (John 19:14).

Day 6 – Thursday (15th of Nisan): Crucifixion Day (High Sabbath Begins at Sunset)

Matthew 27:1–61; Mark 15:1–47; Luke 23:1–56; John 19:1–42

- Jesus is tried by Pilate, scourged, mocked, and crucified.
- Darkness covers the land from the sixth hour (12 p.m.) to the ninth hour (3 p.m.).
- Jesus dies and is buried before sunset.
- This was not a Friday, but the day before a High Sabbath (John 19:31), beginning at sunset.

Day 7 – Friday (16th of Nisan): High Sabbath (Passover Feast)

Leviticus 23:5–7; Exodus 12:16

- A special Sabbath day: no work was allowed.
- Jesus 'body rests in the tomb.
- The women prepare spices before the regular Sabbath (Luke 23:56).

Day 8 – Saturday (17th of Nisan): Weekly Sabbath

Luke 23:56

- The women rest on the Sabbath according to the commandment.
- Jesus is still in the tomb.

Day 9 – Saturday Evening (Start of Sunday, 18th of Nisan): Resurrection!

Matthew 28:1–6; Mark 16:1–6; Luke 24:1–6; John 20:1–18

- Jesus rises after three days and three nights in the grave (Matthew 12:40).
- The tomb is empty early on Sunday morning.
- He first appears to Mary Magdalene.

Summary: Three Days and Three Nights

- Burial: Before sunset on Wednesday (Day 5)
- In the Tomb: Wednesday night → Thursday (Day 6) → Thursday night → Friday (Day 7) → Friday night → Saturday (Day 8)
- Resurrection: After sunset Saturday, at the start of Sunday (Day 9), in perfect fulfillment of Matthew 12:40.

Appendix H: Common Misconceptions About the Crucifixion Timeline

A closer look at one of the most misunderstood aspects of the Passion Week—the timing of Jesus 'death, burial, and resurrection—and how long-standing traditions, especially those shaped by early church practices and Roman influence, have clouded biblical clarity.

Misconception #1: Jesus was crucified on a Friday

This belief is primarily based on the idea that Jesus died the day before a Sabbath (Mark 15:42), and since the weekly Sabbath falls on Saturday, many have assumed He was crucified on Friday.

The Truth:

- John 19:31 clarifies that the following day was not a regular Sabbath, but a High Sabbath—the first day of the Feast of Unleavened Bread (Leviticus 23:6–7), which can fall on any day of the week.
- Jesus died on the Preparation Day (Nisan 14), which that year fell on a Wednesday, just before the High Sabbath began at sunset.

This allows for a literal fulfillment of "three days and three nights" in the tomb (Matthew 12:40).

Misconception #2: Jesus rose on Sunday morning

Because the women found the tomb empty early Sunday morning, many have concluded that Jesus rose at dawn.

The Truth:

- The Gospels never say Jesus rose at sunrise.
- They say the tomb was already empty when the women arrived (Matthew 28:1–6; Luke 24:1–3).
- Jesus rose after sunset on Saturday, which by Jewish reckoning is the beginning of the first day of the week (Sunday).

Misconception #3: There was only one Sabbath that week

This assumption ignores the distinction between weekly Sabbaths and High Sabbaths tied to Jewish festivals.

The Truth:

- That week had two Sabbaths:
    1. A High Sabbath on Thursday (Nisan 15)

2. The regular weekly Sabbath on Saturday

- Luke 23:56 says the women prepared spices before the Sabbath (the High Sabbath) and then rested on the Sabbath (the weekly Sabbath). This would be impossible if there were only one Sabbath.

Misconception #4: Church tradition equals Scripture

The idea of a Friday crucifixion and Sunday morning resurrection became solidified due to early Roman Catholic tradition, not direct biblical teaching. The desire to align the Passion with Roman holy days (e.g., "Good Friday") led to theological compromise.

The Truth:

- Scripture, not tradition, is our final authority (2 Timothy 3:16–17).
- The Catholic Church's calendar contributed to global misunderstanding, but careful study of the Gospels and the Jewish calendar reveal the true sequence of events.

Conclusion: Why This Matters

Understanding the correct timeline of Jesus 'death and resurrection matters because:

- It affirms the accuracy of God's Word down to the very hour (John 19:14).
- It upholds Jesus 'own prophecy of being in the heart of the earth three days and three nights (Matthew 12:40).
- It restores awe and confidence in the sovereignty of God in orchestrating every detail of redemption.

Appendix I: Key Prophecies Fulfilled During Passion

Week

One of the most powerful proofs of Jesus as the Messiah is the staggering number of Old Testament prophecies He fulfilled during the final week leading to His crucifixion and resurrection. These were written hundreds of years before His birth, and yet they unfold in breathtaking accuracy during Passion Week.

1. The Triumphal Entry

Prophecy:

"Rejoice greatly, O daughter of Zion! ... behold, your King is coming to you; righteous and having salvation is He, humble and mounted on a donkey."

—Zechariah 9:9

Fulfillment:

"Jesus found a young donkey and sat on it, just as it is written..."

—John 12:14–15

(Matthew 21:4–9; Mark 11:7–10; Luke 19:35–38)

2. Rejection by His Own People

Prophecy:

"He was despised and rejected by men... He came to His own, and His own people did not receive Him."

—Isaiah 53:3; John 1:11

Fulfillment:

The religious leaders plotted to kill Him, and the crowds who once cried "Hosanna" would later shout "Crucify Him!" (Luke 23:21).

3. Betrayal by a Close Friend for 30 Pieces of Silver

Prophecy:

"Even my close friend in whom I trusted, who ate my bread, has lifted his heel against me."

—Psalm 41:9

"They weighed out as my wages thirty pieces of silver." —Zechariah 11:12–13

Fulfillment:

Judas betrayed Jesus for 30 silver coins (Matthew 26:14–16), and later the money was used to buy the potter's field (Matthew 27:3–10).

4. Silent Before His Accusers

Prophecy:

"He was oppressed, and He was afflicted, yet He opened not His mouth..."

—Isaiah 53:7

Fulfillment:

"But Jesus remained silent."

—Matthew 26:63; 27:12–14

5. Scourging and Beating

Prophecy:

"I gave My back to those who strike, and My cheeks to those who pull out the beard..."

—Isaiah 50:6

"... by His stripes we are healed." —Isaiah 53:5

Fulfillment:

Jesus was flogged, mocked, and struck by Roman soldiers (Matthew 27:26–30; Mark 15:15–19).

6. Pierced Hands and Feet, Crucifixion

Prophecy:

"... they have pierced my hands and feet..."

—Psalm 22:16

"They will look on Me whom they have pierced." —Zechariah 12:10

Fulfillment:

Jesus was crucified—nails driven into His hands and feet (John 20:25–27; Luke 24:39–40).

7. Casting Lots for His Garments

Prophecy:

"They divide my garments among them, and for my clothing they cast lots."

—Psalm 22:18

Fulfillment:

Roman soldiers cast lots for Jesus 'tunic (John 19:23–24).

8. No Bone Broken

Prophecy:

"... not one of His bones will be broken."

—Psalm 34:20

"They shall leave none of it until the morning, nor break a bone of it..."

—Exodus 12:46 (Passover lamb)

Fulfillment:

Soldiers broke the legs of the others crucified, but not Jesus, as He was already dead (John 19:33–36).

9. Buried with the Rich

Prophecy:

"They made His grave with the wicked and with a rich man in His death..."

—Isaiah 53:9

Fulfillment:

Jesus buried in Joseph of Arimathea's new tomb (Matthew 27:57–60).

10. Resurrection on the Third Day

Prophecy:

"You will not abandon my soul to Sheol, or let Your Holy One see corruption."

—Psalm 16:10

"After two days He will revive us; on the third day He will raise us up..."

—Hosea 6:2

Fulfillment:

Jesus rose the third day, just as He foretold (Luke 24:6–7; 1

Corinthians 15:3–4).

Why It Matters

The fulfillment of these specific prophecies—over 300 in total throughout His life—proves that:

- Jesus is undeniably the promised Messiah.
- The Bible is God-breathed and infallible.
- God orchestrated redemption from eternity past with precision and purpose.

As believers reflect on Passion Week, we are reminded not only of God's love, but also of His sovereign power, faithfulness to His Word, and the certainty of Christ's return.

Appendix J: A Chronological Timeline of Passion Week Events

This timeline aligns Jesus 'final week with both Jewish reckoning of days (evening to evening) and key Scriptural references, offering a theologically sound view distinct from traditional interpretations, including the commonly held but inaccurate "Friday crucifixion" view. This sequence reflects Scripture faithfully and highlights the fulfillment of prophecy with clarity.

Day 1 – The Triumphal Entry (10th of Nisan)

Jewish Day: Begins Saturday evening → ends Sunday evening Gregorian Equivalent: Sunday Key

Events:

- Jesus enters Jerusalem riding a donkey (Matthew 21:1–11; Zechariah 9:9)
- The people cry out "Hosanna!"

- He weeps over Jerusalem (Luke 19:41–44)

Day 2 – Cleansing of the Temple

Jewish Day: Sunday evening → Monday evening Key Events:

- Jesus curses the fig tree (Matthew 21:18–19)
- He cleanses the temple, driving out the money changers (Mark 11:15–18)

Day 3 – Teaching in the Temple & Debates

Jewish Day: Monday evening → Tuesday evening Key Events:

- The withered fig tree is noticed (Mark 11:20–21)
- Jesus teaches in parables, confronts religious leaders
- He gives the Olivet Discourse (Matthew 24–25)
- Prediction of the destruction of the Temple

Day 4 – Rest & Anointing at Bethany (Likely Day of Judas 'Plot)

Jewish Day: Tuesday evening → Wednesday evening Key Events:

- Jesus anointed at Bethany in the house of Simon the leper (Mark 14:3–9)
- Judas goes to the chief priests to betray Jesus (Matthew 26:14–16)
- This is two days before the Passover (Mark 14:1–2)

Day 5 – The Last Supper & Gethsemane (14th of Nisan)

Jewish Day: Wednesday evening → Thursday evening Key Events:

- Preparation for the Passover meal (Luke 22:7–13)

- The Last Supper and institution of the New Covenant (Luke 22:14–20)
- Jesus washes the disciples 'feet (John 13)
- Peter's denial foretold
- Agony and prayer in Gethsemane (Matthew 26:36–46)
- Betrayal and arrest (Matthew 26:47–56)
- Taken to Caiaphas and the Sanhedrin

Day 6 – Trial, Crucifixion, and Burial (Still 14th of Nisan)

Jewish Day: Thursday evening → Friday evening Key Events (during the daylight hours):

- Jesus stands before Pilate and Herod (Luke 23)
- He is scourged, mocked, and led to Golgotha
- Crucified at the third hour (9:00 AM)
- Darkness from the sixth to the ninth hour (12:00–3:00 PM)
- Jesus dies and the veil is torn (Matthew 27:50–51)
- Buried before sunset—the beginning of the High Sabbath, the First Day of Unleavened Bread (John 19:31)

Day 7 – The High Sabbath (15th of Nisan)

Jewish Day: Friday evening → Saturday evening Key Events:

- Disciples rest according to the commandment (Luke 23:56)
- Guards are stationed at the tomb (Matthew 27:62–66)
- This is not the regular Sabbath, but a High Sabbath (John 19:31;

Leviticus 23:6–7)

Day 8 – Weekly Sabbath Ends / Resurrection (16th of Nisan)

Jewish Day: Saturday evening → Sunday evening Key Events:

Jesus rises after sunset on the Sabbath, fulfilling "three days and three nights" (Matthew 12:40)

- Mary Magdalene comes to the tomb early "while it was still dark" (John 20:1)
- Jesus appears to her and later to the other women and disciples

Why This Timeline Matters:

- Jesus did not die on Friday, as traditionally taught, but on Wednesday evening to Thursday daytime, fulfilling the Passover lamb typology and the three days and three nights prophecy.
- This timeline harmonizes all Gospel accounts, Jewish festivals, and Old Testament types, reinforcing that God's plan was precise to the hour.

Appendix K: Greek Word Studies from the Passion of Christ

To deepen our understanding of the Passion of Christ, this appendix explores key Greek words used in the Gospel accounts. These terms reveal layers of meaning that are often missed in translation but are vital for grasping the gravity, purpose, and power of Jesus 'suffering, death, and resurrection.

1. Agapē (ἀγάπη) & Phileō (φιλέω)

Reference: John 21:15–17

In Jesus 'restoration of Peter, two different Greek words for "love" are used:

- Agapē (ἀγάπη): Divine, unconditional love—a love of the will and purpose.
- Phileō (φιλέω): Brotherly love or deep affection—emotional love or friendship.

Significance:

Jesus asked Peter twice, "Do you love (agapāō)Me?" and Peter responded, "You know I love (phileō) You." On the third time, Jesus came down to Peter's level and asked, "Do you phileō Me?"—to which Peter answered again with phileō. This powerful interaction shows the gentleness of Jesus, restoring Peter without condemnation but with truth and grace, meeting him where he was.

2. Teleō (τελέω) & Tetelestai (τετέλεσται)

Reference: John 19:30

- Tetelestai is the perfect passive form of teleō, meaning "It is finished" or "paid in full."

Significance:

This is not merely a declaration that His suffering was over—it is a legal and redemptive declaration that the debt of sin has been fully satisfied. The perfect tense shows that the effect of that finished work continues forever. The cross was the fulfillment of all the righteous requirements of the Law and the prophets.

3. Barabbas (Βαραββᾶς)

Reference: Matthew 27:16

The name Barabbas comes from Bar (son) + Abba (father)—meaning "son of the father."

Significance:

A guilty man named "son of the father" was released while the true Son of the Father was condemned. This substitution reveals the Gospel in a single scene: the innocent takes the place of the guilty

4. Ekpneō (ἐκπνέω) "–He Breathed His Last"

Reference: Mark 15:37, Luke 23:46

- Ekpneō means "to breathe out," signifying a voluntary act of yielding up one's spirit.

Significance:

Jesus did not die as a victim of Roman execution alone—He laid down His life (John 10:18). His death was a conscious surrender.

5. Dikaios (δίκαιος) "–Righteous"

Reference: 1 Peter 3:18

- Dikaios means just, righteous, or innocent.

Significance:

Christ, the "just" (dikaios), died for the "unjust" (adikos), to bring us to God. The substitutionary nature of Jesus 'suffering is emphasized by this contrast of guilt and innocence.

6. Skandalon (σκάνδαλον) "–Stumbling Block"

Reference: 1 Corinthians 1:23

- Skandalon originally referred to a trap-stick or a cause of offense.

Significance:

The cross was a scandal to the Jews and foolishness to the Greeks. But to those who are called, it is the power of God and the wisdom of God.

The cross offends pride and self-righteousness, but it opens the door to grace and salvation.

7. Hēlios (ἥλιος) & Skotos (σκότος) "–Sun" and "Darkness"

Reference: Luke 23:45, Matthew 27:45

- Hēlios is the sun.
- Skotos is deep darkness or obscurity.

Significance:

When the sun was darkened during the crucifixion, it was not just a cosmic event—it was symbolic of judgment. Just as darkness fell over Egypt before the Exodus, darkness fell over Jerusalem during the death of the true Lamb of God.

Appendix L: Fulfilled Prophecies in the Passion of Christ

One of the strongest affirmations of Jesus as the Messiah is the precise fulfillment of Old Testament prophecies during His suffering, death, and resurrection. These were written centuries before Christ and fulfilled in detail during Passion Week, proving that Jesus 'death was not a tragic accident—it was God's divine plan from eternity.

1. Betrayed by a Friend

Prophecy:

"Even my close friend in whom I trusted, who ate my bread, has lifted his heel against me."

—Psalm 41:9

Fulfillment:

"Then Judas Iscariot, who was one of the twelve, went to the chief

priests..."

—Mark 14:10

2. Sold for Thirty Pieces of Silver

Prophecy:

"So, they weighed out for my wages thirty pieces of silver." — Zechariah 11:12

Fulfillment:

"They paid him thirty pieces of silver." —Matthew 26:15

3. Silent Before His Accusers

Prophecy:

"He was oppressed and afflicted, yet He opened not His mouth." — Isaiah 53:7

Fulfillment:

"But Jesus remained silent." —Matthew 27:12–14

4. Beaten and Spat Upon

Prophecy:

"I gave my back to those who strike, and my cheeks to those who pull out the beard; I hid not my face from disgrace and spitting."

—Isaiah 50:6

Fulfillment:

"Then they spit in His face and struck Him..."

—Matthew 26:67

5. Hands and Feet Pierced

Prophecy:

"... they have pierced my hands and feet." —Psalm 22:16

Fulfillment:

"They crucified Him ... " —Luke 23:33

6. Crucified with Criminals

Prophecy:

"He was numbered with the transgressors." —Isaiah 53:12

Fulfillment:

"Two others, who were criminals, were led away to be put to death with Him."

—Luke 23:32

7. Mocked by Spectators

Prophecy:

"They wag their heads, saying, 'He trusts in the LORD; let Him deliver Him!'"

—Psalm 22:7–8

Fulfillment:

"They hurled insults, shaking their heads, saying, 'He trusts in God.

Let God rescue Him now if He wants Him ... '"

—Matthew 27:39–43

8. Gall and Vinegar Offered

Prophecy:

"They gave me gall for my food, and for my thirst they gave me vinegar to drink."

—Psalm 69:21

Fulfillment:

"They gave Him wine mixed with gall to drink..." —Matthew 27:34

9. Lots Cast for His Garment

Prophecy:

"They divide my garments among them, and for my clothing they cast lots."

—Psalm 22:18

Fulfillment:

"They divided His garments, casting lots..." —Matthew 27:35

10. Not One Bone Broken

Prophecy:

"He keeps all His bones; not one of them is broken." —Psalm 34:20 (see also Exodus 12:46)

Fulfillment:

"They did not break His legs..." —John 19:33

11. Pierced Side

Prophecy:

"They shall look on Me whom they have pierced." —Zechariah 12:10

Fulfillment:

"One of the soldiers pierced His side with a spear..." —John 19:34

Buried with the Rich

Prophecy:

"They made His grave with the wicked, and with a rich man in His death..."

—Isaiah 53:9

Fulfillment:

"... a rich man from Arimathea named Joseph... took the body and laid it in his own new tomb."

—Matthew 27:57–60

Raised on the Third Day

Prophecy:

"...you will not abandon my soul to Sheol, or let your Holy One see corruption."

—Psalm 16:10

Fulfillment:

"He is not here, for He has risen, as He said." —Matthew 28:6

Each of these fulfillments gives overwhelming evidence of God's sovereign hand guiding the events of Passion Week. The crucifixion of Jesus was not a tragedy—it was a triumph planned from eternity.

Appendix M: Jewish Calendar vs. Gregorian Calendar — The True Timeline of the Passion Week

To understand the true chronology of Jesus 'suffering, death, and resurrection, we must look through the lens of the Jewish calendar, not the Gregorian calendar used today. Many traditional beliefs—such as Jesus being crucified on a Friday and rising on Sunday—are based on church traditions rather than Scripture and the Hebraic context. But the Bible gives us clear and consistent markers if we pay close attention.

Understanding the Jewish Day

- A Jewish day begins at sunset (approximately 6:00 PM) and ends at the following sunset.
- Genesis 1:5 — "And there was evening and there was morning, the first day."
- Therefore, Tuesday at sunset is already Wednesday on the Jewish calendar.

The Key Feasts of the Passion Week

1. Passover (Pesach): 14th day of the Hebrew month Nisan.
2. Feast of Unleavened Bread: Begins on the 15th of Nisan, a High Sabbath (John 19:31).
3. Weekly Sabbath: Always on the 7th day of the week (Saturday).
4. Jesus died on the day of preparation before the High Sabbath, not the weekly Sabbath.

Jesus 'Prophecy: Three Days and Three Nights

"For as Jonah was three days and three nights in the belly of the great fish, so will the Son of Man be three days and three nights in the heart of the earth."

—Matthew 12:40

This cannot be reconciled with a Friday crucifixion and Sunday morning resurrection.

The True Passion Week Timeline (Based on the Jewish Calendar)

Day	Jewish Calendar Day	Event	Scripture
Tuesday (Evening)	Start of 14th Nisan	Last Supper	Matthew 26, Mark 14
Wednesday (Daytime)	Still 14th Nisan	Crucifixion and burial before sunset	John 19:31, Luke 23:54
Thursday (Evening-Day)	15th Nisan High Sabbath	1st day in the tomb	Leviticus 23:6-7, John 19:31
Friday (Evening-Day)	16th Nisan	2nd day in the tomb	Mark 16:1 (after Sabbath women bought spices)
Saturday (Evening-Day)	17th Nisan Sabbath	3rd day in the tomb; resurrection occurs after sunset	Matthew 28:1
Sunday Morning	Beginning of 18th Nisan	Tomb discovered empty; Jesus already risen	John 20:1, Matthew 28:5-6

When Did Jesus Rise?

- Jesus rose after sunset on Saturday, which is the beginning of the first day of the week (Sunday) according to the Jewish calendar.
- The women came to the tomb early Sunday morning, and He had already risen.
- This aligns with three full days and three nights in the tomb:
    - Wednesday sunset–Thursday sunset (1st day)
    - Thursday sunset–Friday sunset (2nd day)
    - Friday sunset–Saturday sunset (3rd day)

Why the Friday-Sunday Tradition is Incorrect

- It only accounts for 1 full day and 2 nights at best.
- It contradicts Jesus 'own words and prophetic patterns.
- The confusion arises from misunderstanding the "Sabbath" mentioned in John 19:31, which refers to a High Sabbath, not the weekly one.

High Sabbath vs. Weekly Sabbath

"...that Sabbath was a high day..." —John 19:31

Greek: megalē hē hēmera tou sabbatou — "a great day of Sabbath"

This High Sabbath was the first day of Unleavened Bread (15th Nisan), regardless of what day of the week it fell on.

The Truth Sets Us Free

The correct timeline restores the power and beauty of God's prophetic precision. Jesus fulfilled the Feasts of the LORD exactly as outlined in Leviticus 23—down to the hour. This should build our faith and anticipation for the fulfillment of the remaining feasts when He returns in glory.

Appendix N: The Seven Sayings of Jesus from the Cross

In His final hours on the cross, Jesus spoke seven powerful statements, each carrying deep spiritual, prophetic, and emotional meaning. These were not random words. Each saying reveals His heart, His mission, and His final offering of love, truth, and fulfillment.

As you read these, allow them to penetrate your heart. They are windows into the suffering, victory, and divine love of the Son of God.

1. Father, forgive them, for they do not know what they do."

Luke 23:34

Even while nailed to the cross, Jesus was interceding—not cursing but forgiving. He was fulfilling the prophecy of Isaiah 53:12, which said He would "make intercession for the transgressors." This is divine mercy at its peak: the Judge dying for the judged.

Reflection: Can we forgive those who wound us when we are still bleeding?

2. Truly, I say to you, today you will be with Me in paradise."

Luke 23:43

This said Jesus to the repentant thief. While the world rejected Him, a dying criminal believed— and received eternal hope. No ritual. No delay. Just grace.

Greek Note: Paradeisos – a word meaning a garden, often symbolic of Eden restored. Jesus was promising immediate spiritual fellowship.

Reflection: It is never too late to turn to Jesus, even with your last breath.

3. Woman, behold your son!" Then He said to the disciple, "Behold your mother!"

John 19:26–27

Jesus, in pain and nearing death, still thought of His mother. He honored her by entrusting her to John's care. Even in suffering, love governs His actions.

Reflection: True discipleship means caring for others, even in your darkest hour.

4. My God, My God, why have You forsaken Me?"

Matthew 27:46; Mark 15:34

This cry echoes Psalm 22:1, a prophetic psalm describing the crucifixion centuries before it happened. In this moment, Jesus bore the full weight of sin. The fellowship He had eternally shared with the Father broken—so ours could be restored

Greek Word: Eli, Eli, lama sabachthani – a mixture of Hebrew and Aramaic, emphasizing agony and fulfillment of prophecy.

Reflection: Jesus was forsaken so you never have to be.

5. I thirst."

John 19:28

Fulfilling Psalm 69:21, Jesus experienced the agony of dehydration and physical torment. But this also signaled the nearing completion of His mission. It shows His full humanity. The Creator became vulnerable.

Reflection: Are we thirsty for the One who thirsted for us?

6. "It is finished."

John 19:30

This is not a cry of defeat but of triumph. The Greek word used is "Tetelestai," meaning paid in full. The debt of sin was canceled. The mission was done. The veil was torn.

Greek Note: Tetelestai was often stamped on legal documents to indicate full payment.

Reflection: There is nothing left for you to earn. Jesus paid it all.

7. "Father, into Your hands I commit My spirit."

Luke 23:46

Jesus voluntarily gave up His spirit. He was in control until the end. This was a quote from Psalm 31:5, a prayer of trust. He who once cried out in forsakenness now returns to the Father in peace.

Reflection: Can we entrust our lives to God, even in death?

Final Reflection:

Each saying reveals Jesus as Savior, High Priest, Son of Man, Son of God, and Redeemer. He spoke as one who fulfilled prophecy, forgave sinners, honored family, and paid the price in full.

These words are not just history. They are living truth—an invitation to believe, to repent, and to enter in the victory He bought on the cross.

Appendix O: The Feasts of the LORD Fulfilled in Christ

God set up seven appointed feasts in the Law of Moses (Leviticus 23). These were not just rituals—they were prophetic shadows of things to come, in Jesus Christ. Each feast carries profound meaning and reveals God's redemptive plan from the cross to the Second Coming.

1. Passover (Pesach)

Leviticus 23:4–5 | Fulfilled in: Jesus 'Crucifixion

- Old Covenant Meaning: Commemorated the night Israel was delivered from Egypt by the blood of the lamb.
- Fulfillment: Jesus, the Lamb of God, was crucified at the exact time Passover lambs were being slain (John 1:29, 1 Corinthians 5:7).

Reflection: Just as the blood of the lamb saved Israel from death, the blood of Jesus saves us from eternal death.

2. Unleavened Bread

Leviticus 23:6–8 | Fulfilled in: Jesus 'Burial

- Old Covenant Meaning: Seven days of eating bread without

leaven (symbol of sin), signifying purity.

- Fulfillment: Jesus, sinless and pure, was buried on the Feast of Unleavened Bread. His body, like unleavened bread, was without corruption (Acts 2:31).

Reflection: His burial marked the removal of sin from our lives. We are called to walk in holiness.

3. Firstfruits

Leviticus 23:9–14 | Fulfilled in: Jesus 'Resurrection

- Old Covenant Meaning: Offering of the first sheaf of the harvest as a sign of what was to come.

- Fulfillment: Jesus rose from the dead on the day of Firstfruits (1 Corinthians 15:20–23). He is the firstfruits of those who have fallen asleep.

Reflection: His resurrection guarantees ours. What began with Him will be completed in us.

4. Feast of Weeks (Pentecost / Shavuot)

Leviticus 23:15–22 | Fulfilled in: The Outpouring of the Holy Spirit

- Old Covenant Meaning: A harvest celebration 50 days after Firstfruits, also commemorating the giving of the Law at Sinai.

- Fulfillment: On the 50th day, the Holy Spirit was poured out (Acts 2). The Church was born. Instead of the Law written on tablets, the Spirit wrote God's law on human hearts (Jeremiah 31:33).

Reflection: This is the power to live holy, preach the gospel, and walk in spiritual authority.

5. Feast of Trumpets (Yom Teruah)

Leviticus 23:23–25 | Yet to Be Fulfilled: The Rapture / Return of Christ

- Old Covenant Meaning: A day of blowing trumpets, calling the people to awaken and prepare for judgment.
- Future Fulfillment: Symbolic of the return of Christ when the trumpet will sound and the Church will be caught up (1 Thessalonians 4:16–17; 1 Corinthians 15:52).

Reflection: Live ready. The trumpet can sound at any moment.

6. Day of Atonement (Yom Kippur)

Leviticus 23:26–32 | Yet to Be Fulfilled: Israel's National Repentance

- Old Covenant Meaning: The high priest made atonement for all Israel once a year.
- Future Fulfillment: Points to the future repentance and salvation of Israel at the return of Christ (Zechariah 12:10; Romans 11:26–27).

Reflection: Jesus is our great High Priest. His atonement is eternal and complete for all who believe.

7. Feast of Tabernacles (Sukkot)

Leviticus 23:33–44 | Yet to Be Fulfilled: The Millennial Reign of Christ

- Old Covenant Meaning: Celebrated God's provision and presence as Israel dwelled in temporary shelters in the wilderness.
- Future Fulfillment: Symbolic of the Messianic Kingdom, where Jesus will reign on earth and God will dwell with His people (Revelation 21:3–4; Zechariah 14:16).

Reflection: The final feast reminds us that we are pilgrims now—but one day, He will tabernacle with us forever.

Summary Table

Feast	Fulfillment in Christ	Status
Passover	Jesus'Death	Fulfilled
Unleavened Bread	Jesus'Burial	Fulfilled
Firstfruits	Jesus'Resurrection	Fulfilled
Pentecost	Holy Spirit Given	Fulfilled
Trumpets	Return of Christ (Rapture)	Awaiting Fulfillment
Day of Atonement	Israel's Repentance at Christ's Return	Awaiting Fulfillment
Tabernacles	Millennial Reign / God with Man	Awaiting Fulfillment

Final Reflection:

The feasts are not relics of the past—they are a timeline of God's redemptive plan, centered on Jesus. As four have been fulfilled with exact precision, we can rest assured the final three will be fulfilled just as surely. Watch. Wait. Be ready.

Appendix P: Were There More Than Two Crucified with Christ?

A Scriptural and Linguistic Examination of a Forgotten Detail

For centuries, Christian tradition has depicted Jesus crucified between two men—one on His right and one on His left. But a closer look at the Gospel accounts, the Greek text, and chronological clues reveals a compelling possibility: there may have been four others crucified alongside Him—two criminals and two robbers, making a total of five crosses at Calvary.

1. The Traditional View: Two Thieves

Matthew 27:38 and Mark 15:27 record:

"Then were there two robbers crucified with Him, one on the right hand, and the other on the left."

- The Greek word used is lēstai (λησταί) — meaning violent robbers, rebels, or insurrectionists.
- Both are said to revile Jesus (Matt. 27:44).

2. Luke's Account: Two Criminals

Luke 23:32–33 says:

"There were also two others, malefactors, led with Him to be put to death."

- The Greek word here is kakourgoi (κακοῦργοι) — meaning evildoers or criminals.
- In Luke 23:39–43, one of them mocks, but the other defends Jesus and believes, receiving the promise of Paradise.

3. The Timing and Sequence

- Luke says the criminals were "led with Him" — meaning they were crucified at the same time as Jesus.
- Matthew and Mark, however, suggest the robbers were crucified after:

"Then were two robbers crucified with Him…" (Matt. 27:38)

This difference in sequence may show that the two robbers were brought later, after the first crucifixion of Jesus and the two criminals.

4. A Clue from John's Gospel

John 19:32–33 adds more weight to this idea:

"Then came the soldiers, and brake the legs of the first, and of the other which was crucified with Him. But when they came to Jesus, and saw that He was dead already, they brake not His legs."

- The Greek word allos (ἄλλος) is used here for "other"—often showing another of the same kind, but distinct.
- If there were only two others, this verse could have just said "both." But instead, the distinction implies more than two.

5. Prophetic Language: "In the Midst"

John 19:18 says:

"Where they crucified Him, and two others with Him, on either side one, and Jesus in the midst."

The Greek word mesos (μέσος) — "in the midst" — often implies more than two flanking figures. Compare this to John 20:19 and Revelation 5:6, where Jesus stands "in the midst" of a larger group.

6. A Historical Echo: The Five Crosses of Brittany

In Ploubezere, near Lannion (Côtes-du-Nord, Brittany), a stone monument displays five crosses—a depiction not common in Western art. Some historians and theologians suggest this reflects an older or alternate understanding of the crucifixion scene, one that matches the possibility found in Scripture: Jesus flanked by two criminals and two robbers.

7. A Reconstructed Picture

Jesus at the center.

- To His right and left: the two criminals, crucified with Him.
- Beyond them: two robbers, added afterward, who reviled Him.
- Thus: Five crosses—and only one Savior.

8. Why This Matters

This is not just a historical or academic point—it emphasizes the loneliness and injustice Jesus bore. Surrounded by guilt on every side, even the company of the condemned is layered with rejection. And yet, one criminal believed—a powerful symbol of mercy.

Whether there were three crosses or five, the center cross still holds the Son of God—pierced for our transgressions, crucified for our salvation.

VISUAL APPENDIX

1. Timeline of Jesus' Final Week (Aligned with the Jewish Calendar)

This visual shows the true sequence of events during Jesus' final week, matched with the Jewish calendar and approximate Gregorian dates. It highlights key moments from the Triumphal Entry to the Resurrection, bringing clarity to the prophetic and historical alignment of Passion Week.

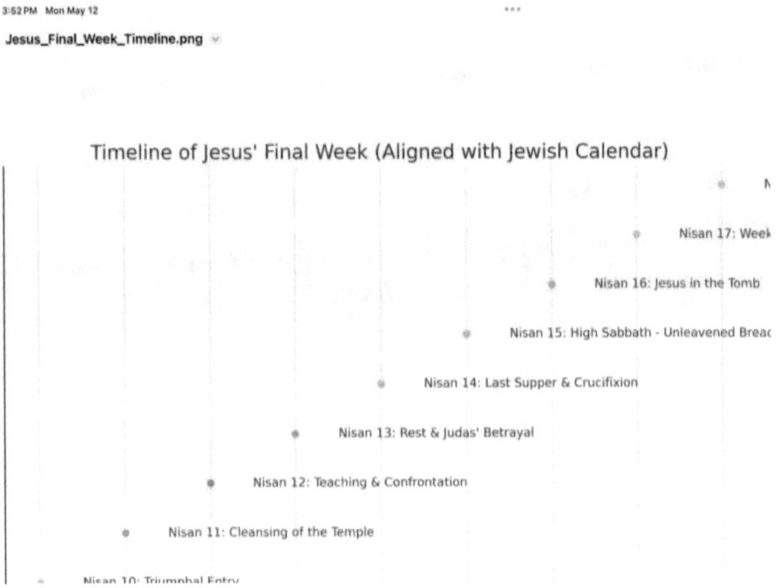

3:52 PM Mon May 12

Jesus_Final_Week_Timeline.png

Timeline of Jesus' Final Week (Aligned with Jewish Calendar)

Nisan 17: Week

Nisan 16: Jesus in the Tomb

Nisan 15: High Sabbath - Unleavened Brea

Nisan 14: Last Supper & Crucifixion

Nisan 13: Rest & Judas' Betrayal

Nisan 12: Teaching & Confrontation

Nisan 11: Cleansing of the Temple

Nisan 10: Triumphal Entry

THE FIVE CROSSES AT

PLOUBEZERE, NEAR LANNION,
Cotes-du-Nord, Brittany.

2. The Five Crosses at Ploubezéré – A Historical

Possibility

This historical image from Brittany, France, depicts five stone crosses, a rare but compelling reminder that there may have been more than two criminals crucified alongside Jesus. According to Matthew 27 and Luke 23, a textual analysis supports the theory that Jesus was crucified between two evildoers, while two robbers were brought later. This visual may support the theory of the two robbers brought later.

www.ingramcontent.com/pod-product-compliance
Lightning Source LLC
Chambersburg PA
CBHW022046050726
47591CB00002B/407

* 9 7 8 1 9 7 2 2 9 9 7 5 3 *